"Chuck Pierce has proven his call as a major prophet over the years. Each prophet has a special anointing and calling. Chuck's special anointing is to know the times and seasons of God that reveal a special purpose God wants to fulfill on the earth. This book is very timely. Every Christian needs to read this book to be able to participate in what God is about to do mightily in His Church and Kingdom. God bless you, Chuck, for hearing from heaven and keeping us in step with God's timing and purpose."

Bishop Bill Hamon, Christian International Apostolic Network; author, *The Day of the Saints*, *Seventy Reasons for Speaking in Tongues* and many others

"As one of the world's most trusted prophets, Chuck writes and speaks with amazing clarity and authority. In *A Time to Triumph: How to Win the War Ahead*, he approaches the future in the same manner in which he approaches all of life: not *if* we can triumph in every situation but *how*! You *must* read this book."

Dutch Sheets, Dutch Sheets Ministries

"The kingdom of God is not in retreat. It will keep expanding until Jesus returns. Accordingly, now is a time to triumph, as Chuck Pierce says in the title of his new book. Pierce looks at this from every angle, and the book is full of clear instructions for how we and our loved ones can be fully prepared to participate in the exciting advance of the Kingdom. *A Time to Triumph* is an essential tool for every believer today. Be sure to get your copy now!"

C. Peter Wagner, vice president, Global Spheres, Inc.

A TIME TO TRIUMPH

A TIME TO TRIUMPH

HOW TO **WIN THE WAR** AHEAD

CHUCK D. PIERCE

Chosen

a division of Baker Publishing Group
Minneapolis, Minnesota

Published by Chosen Books
11400 Hampshire Avenue South
Bloomington, Minnesota 55438
www.chosenbooks.com

Chosen Books is a division of
Baker Publishing Group, Grand Rapids, Michigan

Printed in the United States of America

Library of Congress Control Number: 2016938475

ISBN 978-0-8007-9808-6

Unless otherwise indicated, Scripture quotations are from the New King James Version®. Copyright © 1982 by Thomas Nelson, Inc. Used by permission. All rights reserved.

Scripture quotations identified ASV are from the American Standard Version of the Bible.

Scripture quotations identified AMPC are from the Amplified® Bible, copyright © 1954, 1958, 1962, 1964, 1965, 1987 by The Lockman Foundation. Used by permission. (www.Lockman.org)

Scripture quotations identified GW are from GOD'S WORD®. © 1995 God's Word to the Nations. Used by permission of Baker Publishing Group.

Scripture quotations identified NASB are from the New American Standard Bible®, copyright © 1960, 1962, 1963, 1968, 1971, 1972, 1973, 1975, 1977, 1995 by The Lockman Foundation. Used by permission. (www.Lockman.org)

Scripture quotations identified NOG are from the Names of God edition of GOD'S WORD®. © 1995 God's Word to the Nations. Used by permission of Baker Publishing Group.

Scripture quotations identified NIV are from the Holy Bible, New International Version®. NIV®. Copyright © 1973, 1978, 1984, 2011 by Biblica, Inc.™ Used by permission of Zondervan. All rights reserved worldwide. www.zondervan.com

Scripture identified NIV1984 taken from the HOLY BIBLE, NEW INTERNATIONAL VERSION®. Copyright © 1973, 1978, 1984 Biblica. Used by permission of Zondervan. All rights reserved.

Scripture quotations identified NRSV are from the New Revised Standard Version of the Bible, copyright © 1989, by the Division of Christian Education of the National Council of the Churches of Christ in the United States of America. Used by permission. All rights reserved.

Scripture quotations identified KJV are from the King James Version of the Bible.

Cover design by Rob Williams, InsideOutCreativeArts

16 17 18 19 20 21 22   7 6 5 4 3 2 1

To the Triumphant Reserve
that is now rising
throughout the earth!

Contents

1

A Prophetic Portal into the Future

The times are a-changing—and we must understand the times!

Through more than thirty years, I have walked in God's destiny for me: to hear Him and communicate what He was saying to a divine people who will ultimately triumph on His behalf in the earth realm. That is what this book is about. As I began writing, I was watching confusion in the world intensify before my eyes. Mass murders, wars, ethnic strife, terrorism, economic turbulence and divisions seemed to increase. I watched as people—Christian, Muslim or overall deranged individuals who have lost the joy of living—grew bitter or embraced bitter-root doctrines and began shooting at others or killing them.

But God! We were created to walk in, hear strategies of, steward and then multiply His glory and the resources of the earth. This is a natural breeding ground for conflict. But He knows all and does nothing without first sharing His will with His prophets.

On January 1, 1984, God began to alert me to shifts in world events. This came by a peculiar visitation of His Spirit while Pam and I were executive directors of a children's home outside Houston. God visited me and outlined strange happenings to come concerning the Soviet Bloc countries. This changed our lives.

After the Lord saw that He could trust me to pursue His purposes on a greater scale, He visited me on January 1, 1986, and revealed in detail changes that would come in ten-year cycles for the next forty years, ending in 2026. His army is being prepared for the battle ahead through these and other revelations that build the faith of His people. The book in your hands covers the next ten years, which I sense are summarized as the *time of triumph*.

You might ask, "Why would He visit you?" My answer to this day is because He does nothing on the earth without first revealing to His prophets what His will is in heaven (Amos 3:6–7). This means He strips away secret plans of the enemy and opens up His overall plan, which eventually leads to the triumph of His people and the return of His Son to reign in the earth. His eyes run to and fro to see whom He may communicate with regarding His ultimate purposes of victory. I love Him, seek Him, walk with Him daily and am available for Him to communicate with. You can, too.

God has also revealed to me His *kairos* time—an opportune, strategic or now time—through the Hebraic calendar. This is appropriate, because our covenant through the blood and Spirit of the Lord Jesus Christ of Nazareth aligns us with Abraham the Hebrew, the one who crosses over. We are meant to always cross over out of adversity. By understanding

God's timing, we defeat the enemy, who changes times and laws to weary our minds (see Daniel 7:25).

In Hebrew, each letter, syllable and word has a distinct meaning, sometimes communicating a picture or sound. I believe that is why God made covenant with mankind in this language. When you examine it closely, you see the deeper meaning. For example, the number 2 in Hebrew is *bet*, which depicts a house. In September 2001, we entered the Hebrew year 5762, a year when history would change the way God's house was to be built. (This was the year of the house in the season of *Samekh*, things coming full circle and into fullness.) Most of us clearly remember the beginning of this Hebrew year because the World Trade Center was destroyed in New York City. I believe the world changed at that time so God's house would come to a new level of understanding and be built differently for the seasons ahead.

When I began to share what God had shown me in 1986—that there was a great war ahead, both physically and spiritually, and that America was key in the war—I was met with resistance. That resistance had hit its zenith by the end of 2000. The Body of Christ had no idea about the years of war to come, nor did they wish to really understand them. I was confronted with the accusation that I was leading the Body in America astray by telling them war was on the horizon. I was also chastised for attempting to help Christians understand they are called to spiritual war for their future.

To help the Body shift into a mindset for war, I wrote *The Future War of the Church* and a number of other books.[1] They are still helpful, because much of what was written to prepare us is now a daily reality. *A Time to Triumph* will show you how to process the war ahead. In the next chapters we will begin to unravel the concept of the war Christians face and why they must fight.

The truth is that for the believer in Christ, the best is always ahead. We have a wonderful promise for our future—the promise of eternal communion with God. The Bible clearly tells us that we should not live on earth with our sights set only on what is temporal; we should have a view of eternity and operate from heaven's perspective. God will give us grace to endure what is going on in our temporal world until we come into the fullness of our eternal destiny, which is with Him. This really is the bottom line. The war will intensify, but the best for God's children lies on the road ahead!

Prophecy Is Key

The key to walking in the fullness of your destiny on earth is prophecy. I live in a prophetic dimension that is not bound by space and time but speaks *into* space and time. Heaven is not controlled by time on the earth; therefore prophecy can penetrate time. This book is written from that prophetic dimension, which was revealed by the Spirit of God to help communicate to His children about their future. We all prophesy, but some prophetic gifts are given to help the Body understand the times they are living in and know when to turn right or left on the road ahead. Some prophecies are for warning and direction; others are released for comfort and encouragement.

Prophecy is simply declaring, decreeing or imparting the mind and heart of God, who rules from the throne room of heaven. Therefore, to give an accurate word of God, we must have both His mind and His emotion. Prophecy can unlock the redemptive purpose of a person, city or nation (including its people). On one hand, it exhorts or builds up; on the other, it tears down so restoration can bring individuals, groups and even places into fullness.

A prophetic declaration communicates God's intent to fulfill His promises to us. Receiving a prophetic word can have a powerful impact on the perception of your prophetic destiny; it can shape your vision for the future and bring you into a deeper understanding of God's heart for your life. Prophecy reveals His love, correction and will. Without prophecy we will lose our way; without a vision we will perish.

Here is a prophetic word to encourage you:

> *This is a time of preparation! I am bringing things up and bringing things down, and setting a straight course for you. I am planning your path. I am causing your path to begin to link with other paths. Be comforted from all the struggle of your past seasons.*
>
> *Look ahead! Allow Me to bring you to the intersection of comfort. Wars are ceasing and changing; new wars are arising. Receive comfort like a healing balm upon your eyes from your last war season. Look ahead, for your path will now begin to illuminate in a new way. The signpost you could not see will now come into plain view. As you advance toward this signpost, the way you should go will become clear. As you go past the intersection called "Comfort," the directional arrow for the place that I call "New" will appear before you.*

Choosing God's Ultimate Plan

When God knit you together in your mother's womb, He had a distinct purpose for your life and a timing for it to be fulfilled. He knew before the foundation of the world the season of your birth. He planned the time for you to fit in the earth realm to influence the world around you. If you are reading this, that time is now!

Our lives are a series of choices. Each day when we arise, our first thought should be, "Choose you this day whom ye will serve" (Joshua 24:15 ASV). Many choose to make the world a better place for generations to come. Others choose to serve themselves, and still others to serve destructive structures and systems that are creating detrimental outcomes in society. These choices are making darkness darker. But those choosing light will dispel the darkness and fear that would love to take hold in the earth.

There are religious wars over ideology, and there are spiritual wars that lead to an abundance of life. If we serve God, we will succeed in the redemptive plan for which He created us. We will be aware of His presence. Jesus said, "Blessed (happy, fortunate, and to be envied) are those servants whom the master finds awake and alert and watching when he comes. Truly I say to you, he will gird himself and have them recline at table and will come and serve them!" (Luke 12:37 AMPC). This is comfort in chaos. In a world filled with confusion and evil, we know that if we seek to serve Him each day, then He will come and serve us. He has prepared a table for us in the midst of our enemies (see Psalm 23:5). This book should help each of us to be found awake and alert by the Master.

We should choose life. By choosing life and being empowered to see life, we are then able to discern both good and evil around us. As the apostle Paul exhorted the church of Thessalonica to understand the opposition that was facing them, we must choose to stay alert and come to know the Spirit of God as the restraining force of evil. By walking in the presence of God, we will know when we deviate from

His ultimate plan. We will also know when the enemy of our souls, Satan, attempts to interrupt the cycle of life in God that we were called to complete in this earth realm. We will discern the spirit of lawlessness that is working in the earth. By knowing Father God as we embrace His Son and learn His Spirit, we will eventually triumph over evil.

You might be reading this book and saying, *I am not sure that I know this God or even understand why I am here.* The very Creator of the universe, however, knows *you*; He has knit you together; knows all of your fibers, comings and goings; and has an incredible plan for your life. Choose today whom you will serve so that your future is assured. If you make a willful choice to know the God who is watching mankind's stewardship of the world—every good and every evil action—you will have a peace to live and do your part to accomplish His plan.

The Changing Horizon

To wage war—and win—we must have a battle plan. God knew that His people needed to develop their hearts and minds for war, so, more than thirty years ago, God began preparing me for this time of war and revealing His plan for the unfolding days ahead. We are a people who can tell the future, which is the *expected end*. This means that we have desires and emotions that are being activated, causing us to anticipate something yet to come. Know that the God of heaven can and does reveal to His people what is to come. You need not be afraid of the future! But you must understand times and seasons and know how to change with the future.

As an artist, I learned that one of the first principles of perspective is to see and define your horizon. Because God

17

created time and is time, He is not bound by time. By communicating with His people, He can shift our horizons, or perspectives, to a different time and space to show us what will be coming. Acts 17:25–28, 30–31 (AMPC) is key to understanding how our faith works in time and space:

> It is He Himself Who gives life and breath and all things to all [people]. And He made from one [common origin, one source, one blood] all nations of men to settle on the face of the earth, having definitely determined [their] allotted periods of time and the fixed boundaries of their habitation (their settlements, lands, and abodes), so that they should seek God, in the hope that they might feel after Him and find Him, although He is not far from each one of us. For in Him we live and move and have our being . . . for we are also His offspring. . . . Now He charges all people everywhere to repent (to change their minds . . .), because He has fixed a day when He will judge the world.

The Scripture above explains how the leading philosophers of Greece were unable to conceive of any real distinction between God and the universe. When that happens, darkness rests on any concept of true worship and interaction of the God who loves mankind. Creation had become the central principle of all true religion and was competing with the transcendental idealism of the day. *But God!* He is the Sovereign Ruler. He holds absolute subjection over all the works of His hands. That includes everything in the earth (see Psalm 24). He presides as royal God over all. He attempts to invade and communicate the best plan for each entity in the earth. This is not fate ruling; we are not in bondage to a *que sera sera* mentality—"what will be, will just be."

Faith has an object. I pray that the object of your faith is the Creator of the universe, the Father of mankind's spirits, who sent His Son to redeem us, align us and refine us for the days when light and darkness clash. He Himself is the giver of all life, all breath, all things. The giver of all surely cannot be subject to the receivers of all. Humans are really one race flowing toward the best He has. Individuals and nations that begin to flow toward the sovereign will of God will flourish. He established their horizons by predetermining their times and places. He can move their horizons so they can see any part of the end from the beginning, receiving His arrangements of divine power, wisdom and love.

If we seek Him, we can find Him outside of any religion holding us captive to this present day. We do not merely exist from day to day but have a future, an expected end, and hope. We have life and motion in Him. We can become part of every movement He initiates. He is not bound by times; therefore, we are not bound by time. We become a prophetic people—and remember, He does nothing without first revealing what He is doing to His prophets.

Of course, He could do everything if He chose to. He is quite capable of shaking and rearranging the earth, just as He said, "Let there be light," and there was light. But there was a condition in the Word of God—us! He created us and placed us in the earth realm to watch after and cultivate His "garden," the earth. To continue to do that successfully, we must follow Him.

Place seems to be important to God. Our function or *sphere of authority* also seems key to receiving all the Lord has for us. Abraham had to follow God's command and leave Ur of the Chaldees before God released the promise and came into covenant agreement with him. Following the will of God, Jesus left heaven for earth to redeem us from the power of sin and death. Can you imagine leaving glory to reveal glory in the midst of chaos? In turn, Jesus said, "Follow Me," and commissioned us to go! There seems to be a destination or place for each of us to serve and reflect our faith in the earth. Jesus said, "I will make you fishers of men"—in other words, "Follow Me, and I will cause you to catch mankind."

As we read in Acts 17, along with place and function, *time* seems to be very important to the Lord. The Lord is not "in" time as we are in time. He *is* time. He knows the end from the beginning, yet He has set us into a timed sequence in the earth according to His plan. He expects us to seek Him during the allotted time He has fixed for our lives.

God Determines Times and Seasons

We must understand the times! In his tremendous book *God's Timing for Your Life*, Dutch Sheets shares the following:

> The word *chronos* refers to the general process of time or chronological time. The word *kairos* refers to the right time, the opportune or strategic time, the now time. . . . I have always completely separated these two concepts—chronological time and the right time—but God has been showing me that this is not accurate. Often, they are simply different phases of the same process. *Kairos*, in many ways, is an extension or continuation of *chronos*. As the processes of God's plans unfold, *chronos* becomes *kairos*. The new is connected to the old and, in fact, is often the result of what happened in the old. *Kairos*, the opportune time, is literally born of *chronos*, the general time. When we're in a nonstrategic general season of life's daily routine, plodding along in the *chronos* time, God doesn't totally start over with a *kairos* season. His overall agenda does not change.

He simply takes us through one phase of a process in which our perseverance and faithfulness have allowed Him to shift us into the next phase—a strategic season.[2]

Do you believe that your life can make a difference if you are at the right place at the right time? *Relentless Generational Blessings* by Arthur Burk reveals how God intends each of us to have a generational impact in this world.[3] This very positive book encourages us to see generational blessings in our families as opposed to the negative traits and failures that seem to derail success. This book discusses how we not only inherit a toxic waste dump we do not deserve (generational curses) but also a gold mine that we have not earned (generational blessings). You should recognize your life as a life of blessings. You should also recognize that the nation you live in has an incredible redemptive blessing.

In the midst of strife and defilement, each generation has a responsibility to bring forth these blessings. That is why we are in the earth. I always define *success* as being at the right place, at the right time, doing the right thing. Therefore, vision will open up to allow God's Kingdom people to advance. God's Kingdom people will not only become successful but also strong and innovative in days ahead. Proverbs 29:18 (AMPC) says, "Where there is no vision [no redemptive revelation of God], the people perish; but he who keeps the law [of God, which includes that of man]—blessed (happy, fortunate, and enviable) is he."

We must have vision. At this time in history God is bringing forth our past, aligning it with our present and opening a window so we have a glimpse of the expected end or future of all that is to come. He did this for Daniel. He did this for John. He is now unlocking much of what they saw that was sealed up and revealing the sealed revelation to us today. God will cycle your times and seasons so you break the power of iniquities and injustices.

The Power of Agreement

In *The Future War of the Church*, Rebecca Wagner Sytsema and I described how God was bridging the gap between heaven and earth and bringing agreement between the two, which would lead to a "third-day Church" whose power is like nothing we have known. To become this Church, we must understand the heavenly realms we encounter as we seek to do the will of God.[4]

The Third Heaven

What we think of as "heaven" is usually the third heaven, as we read in 2 Corinthians 12:2. In the third heaven, God the Father sits on His throne with Jesus seated next to Him; from this vantage point, Jesus both knows intimately the Father's heart and makes intercession for us (see Romans 8:34). Like Jesus, our inheritance in the Lord positions us to sit with Him in heavenly places (see Ephesians 2:6); this is where we receive our marching orders.

In the third heaven, there is no obstruction to the accomplishing of God's will. He makes this possible through the gifts He gave to equip the saints for the work of the ministry and for the building up of the Body of Christ: "He Himself gave some to be apostles, some prophets, some evangelists, and some pastors and teachers" (Ephesians 4:11). He gave these gifts to produce unity of the faith in the knowledge of Himself, and from the throne room in the third heaven, He continues to release revelation so we will not be tossed to and fro by the craftiness and trickery of the enemy. He is also releasing revelation so that we will mature into His headship.

The First Heaven

The universe in which we live, including the earthly realm and heavenly bodies, may be called the first heaven. All that we can see, touch and feel in our physical bodies belongs to this realm. Through Christ's death and resurrection, we on earth have access beyond this universe to the realm of the third heaven, where God is seated. That is what we call prayer.

Psalm 24:1 (ESV) declares, "The earth is the LORD's and the fullness thereof." Thus God also rules the earthly realm. Jesus broke the headship of Satan in this realm by going to the cross and overcoming the grave. He then established a structure on earth whose government was spiritually gifted and whose army was endowed with His power: the Church. The Church is in place to enforce His headship.

The Second Heaven

If we have access to heavenly places through prayer, why then is God's will not always done on earth as it is in heaven? That is where the second heaven comes in. Satan, the "prince of the power of the air" (Ephesians 2:2), rules the second heaven, where his demons contest God's reign and His angels.

Satan is the prince of this *cosmos*, the "world" (see John 12:31; 14:30; 16:11), which he has set up with an enticing glory, giving the *cosmos* the ability to entrap. Thus, in Matthew 4:8, "The devil took [Jesus] up on an exceedingly high mountain, and showed Him all the kingdoms of the world and their glory." Satan is also known as the god of this *age*: "The god of this age has blinded the minds of unbelievers, so that they cannot see the light of the gospel of the glory of Christ, who is the image of God" (2 Corinthians 4:4 NIV1984).

The enemy establishes a demonic hierarchy between us and the third heaven in order to block heaven's will from being done on earth. These are the principalities, powers, rulers of darkness of this age and spiritual hosts of wickedness in the heavenly places of which we read in Ephesians 6:12. Any time we rebel against God or comply with the devil's agenda, this hierarchy gains legal right to block heaven's will on earth. Satan gains access to us and to entire territories through individual and corporate sin. In our individualistic society, we may have trouble grasping that we are corporately held responsible in the eyes of God for society's sin. Satan exploits sin in a territory, just as he does sin in our individual lives and in the generations of our families, to establish strongholds that directly oppose God's plan for that territory.

The existence of these three heavens leads us through cycles of change in both the earth and the heavens. At times the heavens shift, as we read in Psalm 102:25–28:

> Of old You laid the foundation of the earth, and the heavens are the work of Your hands. They will perish, but You will endure; yes, they will all grow old like a garment; like a cloak You will change them, and they will be changed. But You are the same, and Your years will have no end. The children of Your servants will continue, and their descendants will be established before You.

Portals of Glory

When God is ready to express Himself, a portal of heaven opens and we and heaven become one. The past aligns to the present, and then the future opens up. This is where revelation is released, for time loses all of its constraints. We are before the throne, and the Possessor of heaven and earth reveals Himself and His will to us. One of the best examples of a portal is when God came down to meet Abraham and Isaac as Jehovah Jireh (see Genesis 22). He came down at Bethel when Jacob fled Esau (see Genesis 28). He came down again when Jacob returned before crossing into the Promised Land (see Genesis 32). A portal is a place of access. Jacob declared that a "gate of heaven" had opened forever at Bethel. This would link his purpose on earth into eternity.

A portal is an opening for God's presence. You may be exhausted from strife, contention and trials linked to the promise that you have been pursuing. Stop and rest, as Jacob did. "Then he dreamed, and behold, a ladder was set up on the earth, and its top reached to heaven; and there the angels of God were ascending and descending on it" (Genesis 28:12).

In this visitation, God revealed to Jacob that He is Lord of the past, the present and the future. This brought Jacob into a relationship with Him. It caused him to have faith that he could actually grab hold of the promise and blessing that had been spoken over him. It also gave him confidence that he could have a relationship with Holy God, just as his father, Isaac, and grandfather Abraham had.

From this experience, Jacob began to worship God personally by acknowledging that the Lord had been at Bethel with him, even though before that point he could not see Him. He memorialized the place, set up a stone and poured oil on it. He recognized God as provider and desired to give a portion back to the Lord. Our encounters with the Lord cause us to either communicate or give.

In *Worship God!*, Ernest Gentile writes,

With the ladder, God initiated worship. He made a way for men to come before God. Then, Jacob saw angels model the responsive action of a worshiper. The text speaks of the angels ascending first and then descending. Symbolically, the angels showed what must take place in people's lives if they are to be true, successful servants of the Lord. First, having "seen" the heavenly invitation, they ascend the shining staircase through their worship. Then, after being in the presence of God, they descend the ladder back to Earth to perform acts of service. First they go up to meet with God; then they can go down to the world with ministry of service.[5]

Hope Is for Now

Through his encounter at Bethel, Jacob learned to hope in the Lord. Hope has an optimistic outlook without any foundation except trust; that trust produces confidence, and confidence causes us to press into the future. This is because hope is linked with expectation. What we are trusting God for needs to eventually manifest in a touchable form.

Are we just striving for heaven, for the sweet by and by? Is that all there is? What about our destiny while we are still here on earth? There *is* a destiny to fulfill. There *is* more than just grace to endure our circumstances until the Lord calls us to Himself. And God *does* have a wonderful plan for our temporal existence that will flow into our eternal communion with Him. Many things must be rearranged during our lifetimes. Many interruptions, distractions, confrontations and even blockages must be overcome as we advance into the fullness of His plan.

Should we continue to hope through the wars and confusion that abound? The answer is a definite yes! Here on the earth we have still not seen a full manifestation of what God intended the earth to experience. Psalm 24:1 (NOG) declares,

"The earth and everything it contains are Yahweh's. The world and all who live in it are his."

Finding the plan of your life and seeing that plan fully manifest can be a messy process. The order of life is sometimes interrupted so that a new order with greater benefit can be inserted. Daily change becomes a key for eventual victory. Yet even in the midst of drastic changes, we should have great joy in knowing that we are moving toward God's destiny.

In *God's Timing for Your Life*, Dutch Sheets writes,

> Life is a series of changes—a process of going from the old to the new—from chronos to kairos. Growth, change, revival—all are processes. Life is connected. Not understanding this, we tend to despise the chronos times of preparing, sowing, believing and persevering. . . . We're not losing or wasting time, we're investing it. And if we do so faithfully, the shift will come.[6]

God has a future and a hope! He has given us promises for salvation, inheritance and spiritual life, and hell hates them. Hell hates the relationship that we can have with the One who can fulfill all promises, which are His promissory notes on which we can base our future. If hell can discourage us with the confusion of the world, we lose sight of the ultimate call to triumph. God has every intention of fulfilling His promises. The real war becomes a covenant war between each of us and an enemy who does not want us to experience the plan for which we were put on earth. The only way to triumph is through this covenant relationship with the One who knit us together to triumph.

This book is about the war of the coming years. It is also about our ability to communicate with earth's Creator so that we have confidence and peace in the midst of confusion. We will encounter circumstances that we know have been directed by God that will open or close doors. Yet we will learn to know when the enemy is preventing us from proceeding into victory.

Most importantly, we will see how God is speaking today to reveal His future. He is a supernatural God who intervenes through dreams, visions and miracles. He can tell us when to turn left or right. He releases power for us to discern the times and the circumstances that surround us. He will do what is necessary to communicate His will—for example, we may read the Bible and see a pattern that illuminates something in a way that is very appropriate for our lives. God gives vision to those who will hear. He has a portal of communication from heaven into earth. Psalm 19:2–4 shares that day by day He utters speech, and that He sends His communication around the lines of the earth.

As I wrote in *God's Now Time for Your Life*, "Each time we respond to the Lord in obedience [according to His plan], we see progress in the overall fulfillment of our earthly purpose. This process and progression is called prophetic fulfillment."[7] Let Him begin to show you His overall plan for you, your family, your city, your nation and, ultimately, the eternal place that He is preparing for you.

Let your hands be trained for war. Let a triumphant spirit be developed within you. Walk in discernment and redeem the times, for the days are evil. Serve the Lord, those in your life and the earth around you with gladness. When evil surrounds, know that there will always be a way of escape.

From Fellowship to Army

To be victorious in war we need to know our God, ourselves and our enemy. So . . . who are we? What is "the Church"?

In Matthew 16:13–20, when Peter tapped in to who the Lord really is, He responded,

> Blessed are you, Simon Bar-Jonah, for flesh and blood has not revealed this to you, but My Father who is in heaven. And I also say to you that you are Peter, and on this rock I will build My church, and the gates of Hades shall not prevail against it. And I will give you the keys of the kingdom of heaven, and whatever you bind on earth will be bound in heaven, and whatever you loose on earth will be loosed in heaven.
>
> Matthew 16:17–19

The Lord is saying that, through this confession of revelation, He will call out a group who will express His purposes from heaven in the earth realm to the gates of hell. He will give these called-out ones keys of authority to bind and loose, to forbid and permit. They will forbid the purposes of Satan to continue, and they will permit God's full diverse expression of Himself to be seen in the earth.

Many people often confuse the Church with the Kingdom of God. They are not the same. The Kingdom is the overall structure that the Church is attempting to express. The Church exists to see the Kingdom established and operating on earth. In other words, the Church facilitates the Kingdom. In the earth, the Kingdom of God and the kingdom of Satan are at war. The Church operates as the armed forces of God in that war; it is the governing, legislating, mediating force that God has ordained and aligned to accomplish His purposes.

You can see the concept of the Church is one of power, legislation and corporate purpose. As God cultivated a people to enter the Promised Land and face giants, so He is cultivating us. We are a decreeing, demonstrating power in the earth. In *The Worship Warrior*, John Dickson and I write,

"Worship and war go together. But for war we must have an army [who is] organized for battle."[8]

In *The Future War of the Church*, Rebecca Wagner Sytsema and I write,

> The Greek word *ekklesia* ("Church") means those gathered to accomplish something or a group of people who are called out for a purpose. The first time this notion of a people called out appears in the Bible is when the children of Israel come out of Egypt. . . . Even though the people of promise had remained in Egypt for 400 years, they had to be called out in God's perfect time, so that they could journey to the place of the promise's fulfillment.
>
> What did God do to call out His promised people from one place and send them to their destined place of fulfillment? First of all, we see that He changed governments over the people:

>> Now it happened in the process of time that the king of Egypt died. Then the children of Israel groaned because of the bondage, and they cried out; and their cry came up to God because of the bondage. So God heard their groaning, and God remembered His covenant with Abraham, with Isaac, and with Jacob.
>>
>> Exodus 2:23–24[9]

Shifts in civil government serve as a sign of Father God shifting things for His people. We continue,

> This calling-out place is also the first time we see God's heart to order His people for war. . . . "Bring out the children of Israel from the land of Egypt according to their armies" (Exodus 6:26). In other words, the order of the family clans was important for the future of their victories, according to the promises He had ordained for them.

God called the children of Israel out of Egypt because He had planned to govern them Himself. He had ways to govern them, and He raised up the order and method of government for His people so they could accomplish His purposes.[10]

We find this government being extended into the earth with gifts of grace by the Lord Jesus Christ when He was ascending after His death and resurrection. This ascension has brought Him to the right hand of the Father, making Him available to us to legislate God's Kingdom. Ephesians 4:11–16 says,

> And He Himself gave some to be apostles, some prophets, some evangelists, and some pastors and teachers, for the equipping of the saints for the work of ministry, for the edifying of the body of Christ, till we all come to the unity of the faith and of the knowledge of the Son of God, to a perfect man, to the measure of the stature of the fullness of Christ; that we should no longer be children, tossed to and fro and carried about with every wind of doctrine, by the trickery of men, in the cunning craftiness of deceitful plotting, but, speaking the truth in love, may grow up in all things into Him who is the head—Christ—from whom the whole body, joined and knit together by what every joint supplies, according to the effective working by which every part does its share, causes growth of the body for the edifying of itself in love.

In the next two chapters, we will discuss the changing mindset of the Body of Christ. Armies have always been organized in different ways at different times. When we talk about a changing paradigm or wineskin in the Church, we are talking about God's army being organized in a way to express themselves to the dark forces of the age they represent. In *The Worship Warrior*, John Dickson and I share,

Today God is raising up an army of worshiping warriors. No force on Earth will be able to withstand this army. In the New Testament we find this principle: God had His Church, or *ekklesia* group, called out and assembled together as one man. This army was called out to complete the purpose of God in the earthly realm (see Hebrews 8:1–13).

This group was called to worship Him. They also are called to enlist others. They are established under His authority (see Matthew 16:13–21). They have a sure foundation (see Ephesians 2:20). They demonstrate His redeeming death by exercising the power of His resurrection. They know that He is the head. They are members. They fellowship together to gain strength and access the mind of their leader. They are fighting against an enemy and his hierarchy. They are bold witnesses, and they have a hope of their leader's return to fill and restore all things in the earthly realm. They worship unrestrained, so they can obey and further their master's Kingdom plan. They are a Bride ready for war at all times to avenge the enemy and defeat his plan of darkness. Arise, worshiping warriors! Let the Church arise![11]

War means the grace to *fight and triumph*. Throughout this book we will discuss the new wineskin that is necessary for war. We must carry the identity of God for this season to triumph over the cosmos that surrounds us. The world is attempting to mold us into the blueprint of the enemy, who rules the structures of the earth. We must learn, however, to come up higher and build accordingly in Him.

2

Shifting into the War Ahead

The times are a-changing, as Bob Dylan prophetically declared in the 1960s in his famous song. A "Kingdom shift" is taking place around the world, for God always has times of restoration. When He ascended into heaven to be seated next to the Father, He gave gifts to mankind. His purpose was that in each generation these gifts would come into fullness.

I believe the current shift is a Spirit shift, in which the Holy Spirit begins to manifest and demonstrate through the gifts God gives today. If you are a blood-bought believer, you have gifts in your bloodline that are waiting to manifest. If you have yet to surrender your life to the Messiah, even though your spirit man is not yet a conduit for the Holy Spirit and His gifts lie dormant, they are still waiting to come alive.

Bob Dylan sang of what would happen to those who refused to come to terms with the changes happening around them. In these times, if you are fearful, you will find yourself held captive and afraid to press into your future—the expected end that awaits you.

One of my favorite Scriptures revolves around a young woman, Mary, who in short order faced the hovering Spirit of God, angelic forces, relatives experiencing great changes, her betrothed learning she is with child, shepherds seeking her after she births this child and Magi who bring her treasures. Those are lots of shifts and changes for a young girl to process. "But Mary," Luke 2:19 tells us, "kept all these things and pondered them in her heart."

As you read this book, I ask you to ponder what you are reading and what is happening in your environment and in the world. That means to consider it deeply and thoroughly, to meditate upon or weigh it carefully in the mind, to consider it thoughtfully. Ponder what is written here, and then choose your Kingdom alignment for the future.

Be like Mary! You will have much to ponder in the seasons ahead. I hope you will choose to become one of God's triumphant, overcoming testimonies walking the earth.

The End Is Not Yet

Wars have raged for millennia, and we must accept that war is here to stay. Even Jesus said, "And you will hear of wars and rumors of wars. See that you are not troubled; for all these things must come to pass, but the end is not yet" (Matthew 24:6). That means that, even though the world seems to be turbulently changing around you, you can settle down and settle in for war—knowing that our Prince of Peace reigns continually!

The point of this book is that "the end is not *yet*." The next several years will affect generations to come. Some of God's soldiers will pass into eternity while others continue in the war of the ages on earth. Many who read this book and its two companion books, *The Future War of the Church* and *God's Unfolding Battle Plan*, will be glad to have a record of the times that preceded them.

In "The Times, They Are A-Changin'," Prophet Dylan urged those who held power or authority in society—from political leaders to journalists to parents—to keep up with the changing times, lest they become impediments to those willing to embrace what was occurring. He could have been singing about the changes the Church is encountering in these days. For their own good and for the good of those who follow them, Christian leaders have to embrace what the Lord is doing in our day, even if it means turbulence, war and an end to the current Church structure. Dylan's lyrics are almost as timeless as the words of Jesus in Matthew 24:6. The times, they are a-changing—again!

What Is *Shift*?

Because I refer to it throughout this book, I want to expand on the idea of a shift. Transition has three phases: death, confusion and arrival of the new. After periods of change, there comes a time when you leave a transition, or crossing over, from one season to the next. You can get hung up in death or confusion, but the will of God is always for you to shift into the new. At this point, you should no longer prophesy that the new will happen, for the new *is* happening. At that moment, your whole being must make a shift—a change of place, position or direction.

A shift entails a scheduled time and includes an exchange or replacement of one thing for another. It can be described as a change of gear, allowing you to accelerate. A shift can also be an underhanded or deceitful scheme; we must recognize, therefore, that the enemy is plotting to stop the shift the Lord intends for us.

The Body of Christ is currently in a restorative shift that began in the early 1900s. The evangelist began to manifest in the 1950s. In the '60s the pastor-teacher began to teach that a new move of God was coming, culminating in the Jesus Movement. The church structure of that time, however, did not really accept that move or its fruit. The '70s and '80s continued with a charismatic manifestation of gifts known as the Third Wave. Even in more traditional settings, this Third Wave of the Spirit had some liberty. The Spirit of God added to it a renewal and restoration of the prophetic gift. Then, in the late 1990s, God began by His Spirit to restore the apostolic gifting back into His people. This began with a prayer movement to reach all the unreached people groups in the earth. Many believe that we are now in the third great reformation in the earth realm.[1]

Shaking occurs during a shift, just as in a fault line. We either shift ourselves or get caught in a rift, or the place of dividing. God has a time for division when it is necessary for His covenant to come forth in a new way. Jesus said it this way: "I came not to send peace, but a sword" (Matthew 10:34 KJV). Change that produces a shift can also produce rifts in every area mentioned above, especially in relationships. Let's be sure that we in God's Kingdom do not use the sword on each other!

In *Redeeming the Time*, I encouraged us with some simple steps for making the shift that God is requiring now:

- **Develop His mind.** Jesus "made Himself of no reputation, taking the form of a bondservant . . . He humbled

Himself and became obedient" (Philippians 2:5–8). Do not lean on your own understanding; you will never have enough knowledge to make the right choice.

- **Learn to express His heart.** Let the Lord subdue your emotions, commanding self-pity, hope deferred and bitterness to leave.

- **Change your atmosphere.** Speak faith! Break the negative atmospheric presence around you with prophetic declarations of victory.

- **Optimize resources for doing exploits.** Use the resources you have to create new resources or bring them into a new level of fullness.

- **Watch for the "suddenlies."** Be on the lookout for sudden transformation. Hope deferred and weariness will cause you to miss when our Lord moves on your behalf.

- **Learn to cross over.** We must have an "over" mentality: Overcome or be overcome. Also, be sure you are being overseen and define the sphere that you are overseeing.

- **Develop a Kingdom mentality.** The Kingdom advances in victory through violent spiritual conflict (see Matthew 11:12). Fear not! The Church is God's warring agent.

- **Find your new river of joy.** Praise enthrones the Lord in our midst. Do not let upcoming manifestations create a rift that keeps you from experiencing God's Kingdom plan.

- **Experience a shift even if it creates a rift.** For God's covenant plan to shift, a rift drove Abraham and Lot apart. Be willing to separate so you can move forward into new levels of blessings.[2]

The Kingdom Shift

Because we have seen measures of restoration throughout the earth of the ascension gifts in Ephesians 4:11, I would summarize the overall shift that has now occurred as a Kingdom shift. This shift from earth to Kingdom advancement in this age is now creating a great clash of kingdoms. Whether you are fully aware or not, you are shifting, and the world around you is changing. You are part of both the shift and the clash!

You are the subject of some kingdom somewhere. How you operate and position yourself in the kingdom you are submitted in will determine your future. This book will help you determine and accept your positioning and calling. It will assist you in your call to the war ahead, whether spiritually, individually, corporately, nationally, territorially or generationally.

We did Mr. Dylan's song in a church setting and added our own verses about the Kingdom being yours for the taking, but choosing what is safe means forfeiting everything God has for you. My hope is that each of you would decide to be part of God's Kingdom army that will advance and ultimately triumph in the earth. This army has been developing through history and is led by Jesus Christ of Nazareth, who is alive and seated on the throne next to Father God, the ultimate Creator and Ruler of the universe. Jesus came to reveal the heart of the Father to the world, to destroy the works of the enemy of mankind and to develop a triumphant people who will eventually enter into the fullness of earth's destiny. He is known as the *Mashach*, the Anointed One, who breaks the yoke of slavery of mankind and offers each a redemptive plan, beginning with saving grace, to join the triumphant army that eventually rules and reigns.

You might already be asking yourself, *Is God ruling anywhere? I only see war and confusion in the earth intensifying.* Let me suggest that you be open to read and ponder what is written. I am a believer. My worldview and thought processes have matured around the Word of God. By that I am not just referring to the Bible but a *living Word* that I have come to know and form a relationship with.

Clashes of the Future

Let me step back to explain how the Lord propelled me to write this book and two others. When the Lord gave me visions from heaven's throne room in 1984 and 1985, I was not heavily active in the prophetic realm, nor was I looking for divine strategy from God. Yet the vision I received from the Lord on December 31, 1985, forever changed my life. I have written about it in *The Future War of the Church* and *God's Unfolding Battle Plan*, but I feel this vision still remains so applicable that it is worth sharing for those who are not familiar with it.[3]

I had devoted New Year's Eve to reading Scripture and prayer, but instead the Lord nudged me to close my Bible and lay aside my prayer list. Then He began revealing how the Church was to prepare for the future. He showed me that within twelve years, the government of the Church would change to reflect the pattern given when Jesus ascended to heaven; this would release revelation and gifting for new administrative methods that would bring influence and victory to His people. He also revealed an intensifying of conflict that only His Spirit could confront; therefore, His Spirit would have to increase in His people. I saw three distinct governmental structures and their importance for the future of society.

1. The Existing Church Structure

God first showed me the Church as I knew it. (At that time I was a member of a mainline denomination, and I did not really know any other method of doing church.) Its present form appeared as a large building of about fifty stories. Each floor represented a year of development. Each room in the building was brightly lit. The structure was well built and somewhat flexible, and it seemed to be breathing and moving slightly when the wind blew.

As I watched, however, the building became increasingly rigid and unchangeable. As it grew rigid, the lights dimmed, even though some light still emanated from the rooms. The structure began to look more like a prison than a flexible organism of change. And God said,

> I will have an opportune time when many will come out of this Church government and begin to flow into another government structure that will arise! I will have a people who worship Me in spirit and truth, who will have to know My reality to survive. This will be a Kingdom people!

I could see the Kingdom in the Word but not in the worship I was involved in; therefore, the "coming out" portion began to penetrate me. It was clear that the present structure of operation was not to hinder the future of His movement on earth.

2. Adverse Antichrist Governments

God then showed me two other buildings. The first was labeled Militant Religious Governments (the "Isms"). This building was constructed rapidly and had great strength. I saw rooms representing religious systems from around the world, including the United States.

40

In this building, plans for terrorist activity were devised in strategy rooms. These acts of terrorism were designed to breed fear in the target areas—fear meant to compel people to convert to these religious systems and to withhold wealth meant for His Kingdom so that other religions could control it. I also saw the Lord's heart for those ensnared by these religious systems; He longed to see them released and their trapped gifts liberated for Kingdom purposes.

One key religious system was Islam, which was to have great influence on the earth. (Please understand that I am referring to the religious structure of Islam, which is controlled by satanic principalities and powers. I am not talking about the Muslim people per se, whom God loves and for whom Jesus died.) I saw that Islamic religious forces would be positioned in key places throughout the world. The Islamic religious structure follows the spiritual principle of treading to gain territory (see Joshua 1:3): Those enslaved to it gain military control of territories, establishing their authority through war, bloodshed or whatever necessary to secure what they have gained, being willing to "lay their lives down" to advance their agenda.

In front of the Isms I saw another, smaller building called Lawlessness. Here were hidden lawless forces linked with secret societies such as the Ku Klux Klan and Freemasonry. The influence of this building led to lawless acts of violence and murder in schools, churches, shopping malls and supermarkets. The building of Lawlessness was actually connected in form and administration to the religious systems located in the Isms building. The Lord was showing me that the same type of religious spirit controlled both. Lawlessness was the headquarters where all the larger building's operations received their marching orders. They seemed to be connected with something like the vacuum tubes used for making a bank deposit. When a leader from the Lawlessness building went outside, a transaction of evil would be exchanged. I saw governments of the earth being influenced by these structures, some of them trying in vain to resist them with their own strength.

Words then appeared on the foundations of these two buildings: *Mammon, Ashtoreth, Jezebel, Ahab, Babylon* and *Baal*. Next to these were anti-Semitic slogans and Hindu philosophies, among others. Ancient plans were adapted for this age and empowered by illegal bloodshed.

God said that understanding how these structures operated would give us keys for victory when the structures of the Isms and Lawlessness rose up in the future to gain control. He reminded me of how Satan uses times and laws to wear down the saints (see Daniel 7:25).

3. The Church of the Future

Finally God showed me a building filled with light. The Lord called it My Future Kingdom Authority. It was very small, just beginning to form, and was still lacking in size and shape. Even so, the structure was nothing but light and glory. On its foundation appeared the five ascension gifts listed in Ephesians 4.11, which make up the government of God: *Apostles, Prophets, Evangelists, Pastors* and *Teachers*. In the vision, these gifts were placed in the foundation as God brought order to them. Every time a gift was set in order, the light increased tremendously.

Once in order, the gifts became a like a magnet for people; like the early Church, many were added at an exponential rate. (At a later time, God called this group the "triumphant reserve" and showed me in 2008 that they would start arising.)

I saw many leaders from the Existing Church Structure move their offices from the old building to this new structure. As they turned out the lights in their old offices, that building grew darker and much more rigid. It was eventually unable to withstand the Isms and Lawlessness.

As the Lord's new structure grew, however, it superimposed itself over the Isms and Lawlessness and had the ability to overcome their governments. My Future Kingdom Authority was filled with *Kingdom* people who were filled with His glory and light. They were wiser than serpents and shrewder than sons of the world. This people would learn anew how to do exploits in the world.

God then said,

> This is the government of the Church of the future! The people of this government will arise and spread My light throughout the world in the days of the latter wars. This government will overcome all other governments. When this government is in order, you can then command governments of the earth to come into order. This will be the government that My latter-day blessings will rest on. This will be the government in which My glory will be seen. This will be the government that truly comes into a double-portion anointing and will dethrone the systems of Babylon on earth. This government will not be one of compromise but of determined commitment to My purposes. Their voice will be bold and their actions bolder.

After this I saw China, where, the Lord showed me, this transformed Church would first arise. China became in the eyes of the world a rising nation. It is the prototype nation of the coming Kingdom war. (I will discuss this more in later chapters.) This is the apostolic Church, and she is now arising!

43

Receiving the Issachar Anointing

Because I am known as an "Issachar prophet," I want to release an impartation to you. A key for the Church and God's
remnant people is to understand the times in which we live,
just as the tribe of Issachar did. Everything the Lord showed
me when He visited me in 1986, all the change that would
come in ten-year cycles, is happening now! Understanding
the times and seasons is key for victory in our personal lives
and territories, yet most of us do not understand the biblical timetables.

Those belonging to Issachar were different. Issachar was
the Torah tribe: They knew how to "tell time" by skillfully
using the Word of God. First Chronicles 12:32 refers to "the
sons of Issachar who had understanding of the times, to
know what Israel ought to do, their chiefs were two hundred;
and all their brethren were at their command."

God is causing this tribe to rise again in the earth and
be seen in His Kingdom. The Word is not just historical
but living and powerful. Without the Issachar anointing,
we do not have the revelation of present truth today. I
am probably best recognized for this anointing for time
in the Body of Christ, and I have attempted to study to
show myself approved. Actually, one of the most important
keys of my life is that I seem to recognize when I am not
in God's timing.

Issachar was stationed on the east of the Israelites' camp
with Judah and Zebulun, his brothers, and they led the march
in the desert toward the Promised Land (see Numbers 2:1–9;
10:14–15). *Issachar* means "he will bring reward." Men of
Issachar knew how to ascertain the periods of the sun and
moon, the intercalation of months and the dates of solemn
feasts, and they could interpret the signs of the times. In

addition, Jacob prophesied, "Issachar is a strong donkey, lying down between the sheepfolds. When he saw that a resting place was good . . . he bowed his shoulder to bear burdens, and became a slave at forced labor" (Genesis 49:14–15 NASB). We might suppose that Issachar would be snared by comfort rather than war, or that they were prone to move in sun worship instead of prophecy. Yet they had the ability to move in and understand feast times and to position themselves at the right place at the right time. If we are to advance in victory, if we are to carry God's burdens in the earth realm and bring them to birth at the appropriate time, we must have the Issachar anointing.[4]

We also find insight in the order of Issachar's birth relative to his brothers. Issachar was the ninth son of Jacob and the fifth son of Leah. This combination reveals properties found in no other child of Jacob. The Hebrew number nine, *tet*, means to judge, bring to judgment, administer justice, adjudicate, execute judgment, rule or govern. Actually, this number is linked with the concept of goodness.[5] In the New Testament Issachar is linked to the nine fruits of the Spirit and the nine gifts of the Spirit. To know what to do in a situation, we must allow the gift of the Holy Spirit to manifest within us. If we do this, we will profit in all things (see 1 Corinthians 12:7).

The Hebrew number five, *hei*, connotes strength, protection, deliverance and exaltation. The overall concept is receiving grace to help.[6] When the power of grace enters into time, many situations are rearranged. There is not an understanding of the full concept of judgment in the Body of Christ. When God is ending one season and beginning another, or taking us through transition, He has to end or bring to death some old situations. This is why the tribe of Issachar could understand time. They knew how certain structures had to end so that the new season that God had would begin.

As we saw in the Israelite camp, the tribe of Issachar was positioned strategically with Judah and Zebulun. Judah's name meant "may He [God] be praised." His tribe was prophetically destined to go first as the war tribe that would conquer. Zebulun, whose name meant "dwelling" or "habitation," was the tribe of war, ships and trade. Issachar, who could understand the times, marched between them. You can see now why 1 Chronicles 12:32 (AMPC), "And of Issachar, men who had understanding of the times to know what Israel ought to do," had such significance at the time Israel was moving from the government of the house of Saul to the government of the house of David, of the tribe of Judah. The tribes were in a tremendous conflict and transition, and Issachar could give great insight on how to make this shift. Let's look at the distinct characteristics inherent to the tribe of Issachar:

1. **Prosperity.** Issachar's birth came about because of a trade agreement between Leah and Rachel in Genesis 30:14–15. After he was born, Leah called him Issachar, saying, "God has given me my hire" (verse 18, AMPC). The people of the tribe of Issachar would become servants to many, work for wages and live comfortable lives.

2. **Intercession.** Jacob prophesied this characteristic in Genesis 49:14–15 (AMPC), "Issachar is a strong-boned donkey crouching down between the sheepfolds. And he saw that rest was good and that the land was pleasant; and he bowed his shoulder to bear [his burdens]

and became a servant to tribute [subjected to forced labor]." Issachar had the ability to stand between two burdens or two decisions and choose correctly.

3. **Divine Alignment.** The tribe of Issachar moved at home and abroad in its sphere of authority, as we see in Moses' prophecy in Deuteronomy 33:18–19 (NIV), "Rejoice, Zebulun, in your going out, and you, Issachar, in your tents. They will summon peoples to the mountain and there offer sacrifices of righteousness; they will feast on the abundance of the seas, on the treasures hidden in the sand." In other words, Zebulun would trade and Issachar would manage at home what was traded. (See also Isaiah 60:5–6, 16; 66:11–12.)

4. **Ability to Ascertain Seasonal and Immediate Changes in Time.** According to the Targum, an Aramaic translation of the Old Testament, they knew how to interpret not just heavenly bodies but also the calendar and dates of solemn feasts to understand the times and even the land (see Deuteronomy 20:11; 1 Kings 9:21). That is why, for example, we see a company from Issachar coming to the celebration of the Passover when it was restored by Hezekiah (2 Chronicles 30:18).[7] Most of the fertile Valley of Jezreel fell within Issachar's territory; thus Issachar was destined to stand and occupy the place that Ahab and Jezebel ruled.

5. **Awareness of the Anointing.** Isaiah 10:27 says, "The yoke will be destroyed because of the anointing oil." An Issachar type of gifting recognizes what is necessary to break people free from their bondage. If we receive this anointing and remember where we are called to stand, we can see the overthrow of every Jezebel structure that has risen against God's Kingdom plan in our

generation. The danger is that we will lose our sense of timing with our footing or become comfortable in our prosperity and allow Jezebel to take our destined valley.

6. **Understanding of War and Political Change.** We find the tribe Issachar moving with Deborah and Barak in battle. In spite of its reputation for seeking comfort, the tribe fought bravely against Sisera (see Judges 5:15). As Issachar did, I have tried to lead the Body in the quest to understand the political changes we are experiencing and how to abound in the midst of political upheaval and war.

7. **Possession of the Power to Bless.** In the unusual circumstance described in Deuteronomy 27, Issachar was chosen as one of the tribes that could bless what God was blessing. Those who know how to bless get blessed.

Spiritually, Christians should be men and women "knowing the time, that now it is high time to awake out of sleep; for now our salvation is nearer than when we first believed" (Romans 13:11; see also Ephesians 5:16; 1 Peter 4:1–4). We should heed the warning of Jerusalem, which fell "because you did not know the time of your visitation" (Luke 19:44). We should help transfer the Kingdom from Satan to its coming rightful Lord (Luke 19:12–27), for they are truly wise who turn many from the power of Satan unto God (Daniel 12:3; Acts 26:18).[8] Because we are grafted into the covenant of Abraham, and because the fullness of the Jew and Gentile must occur before the Lord returns to the earth to reign, we need to receive this anointing and be like this tribe.

Watchmen Arise!

Not only do we need an Issachar anointing, but we need a watchman anointing as well. The *shamar* watchman-prophet watches for the Lord to perform His Word. Once the Word of God is sent from heaven, we must watch until the performance of the Word occurs.

Our life and destiny are on a continuum. As we move through life, we need to constantly seek new direction and new revelation from God. We cannot just grab hold of one level of revelation and think it is going to ride us through to the end. Ezekiel, the watchman-prophet, demonstrated this when God showed him what he would need to do to see the vision of the valley of dry bones fulfilled (Ezekiel 37). If Ezekiel had stopped at any point before God's full purpose had been accomplished, he would have failed. Ezekiel went through a four-step process at each new level of prophecy. These same four steps we need to follow, if we want to see prophetic fulfillment in our own lives.

1. He received prophetic revelation. Ezekiel sought God and was open to receiving prophetic instruction. In fact, he *expected* God to speak to him. God is speaking to us today! How often in our daily lives do we expect to hear Him? We need to learn to listen for God's voice in order to receive direction for our lives to move us forward.

2. He obeyed the voice of the Lord. God told Ezekiel what to say and what to do in order for the next step to be accomplished. This seems terribly basic, yet it is critical. Ezekiel could not have moved to the last level of prophecy without obeying God at the first, second and third. If you are having difficulty gaining new revelation and hearing the voice of the Lord, be sure that you have done all that the Lord has required of you thus far. For example, if you have fallen out of relationship with someone and the Lord reveals that you have to get right with that person, do not go back to the Lord looking for new revelation until you have obeyed. If you want to move toward prophetic fulfillment, you had better get right with that person.

3. He watched God's purpose being accomplished and assessed the situation. At each level of obedience, Ezekiel saw miracles as God's will was accomplished. Even so, he knew that all of God's purposes had not yet been fulfilled. He saw the bones come together—which in itself must have been a great and miraculous sight—but when he looked closer, he saw that, despite this great miracle, there was no breath in the bones. Then he saw breath come into them and a living, breathing army replacing a dead pile of dry, useless bones. And yet there was still hopelessness and infirmity. It was not until Ezekiel saw the Lord break infirmity and death off of the great army and bring them into the land He had promised them that the process of prophetic fulfillment was complete. Even when we see great miracles along the way, we need to be sensitive to the Holy Spirit's leading as to whether His will has been fully accomplished.

4. He listened for his next instruction. Miracle after miracle did not stop Ezekiel from seeking God for the next step. Ezekiel did not bask in the awesome works of God in a way that prevented him from looking forward. Of course, we need to stop and thank God for His great power and allow ourselves to be drawn into worship. But we cannot let the glory of something that has already occurred keep us from moving toward a greater level of glory. Have you ever tried to walk backward while focusing on where you have just been? Not only is your progress greatly slowed, you are liable to fall on an obstacle that you should have seen.

Elijah saw the heavens shut up without rain for three and a half years. During that time he legislated the heavens, withstood false prophets and did miracles. When the three and a half years ended, his watching had to take action. He then went into intercession mode and called the rain back into the earth realm.

Remember, Jesus "steadfastly set His face to go to Jerusalem" (Luke 9:51). He never got off track in His purposes on earth, and by staying totally focused, He brought redemption to us. We need to keep our eyes focused on what lies ahead and seek God for our next instructions. Even with all of Paul's great accomplishments for the Lord, he writes,

> I do not count myself to have apprehended; but one thing I do, forgetting those things which are behind and reaching forward to those things which are ahead, I press toward the goal for the prize of the upward call of God in Christ Jesus.
>
> Philippians 3:13–14

Paul was reaching toward his prophetic fulfillment.

Dynamics of Change Will Abound

We will have an abundance of changes to watch for in the earth realm in this next season. The Spirit of God will give each of us our assignments in the earth. Here are but a few:

- **We must watch Israel.** This is God's covenant land. The God of Israel will arise to reign in the days ahead, and one new man will also arise in the earth.

- **We must watch the rising conflicting kingdoms.** Goat nations and sheep nations will be determined. We must watch as nations choose their inheritance (see Joel 3). Also, we must understand Gog and Magog, as well as the reality of Russia, China, the Middle East and Africa! How will nations either conform to the world's war and religion or transform in God's Kingdom plan?

- **We need to watch as a triumphant reserve arises.** This triumphant reserve is a covenant people who will be realigned and become one, and they will be known by their love. They will be gathered supernaturally and will carry God's glory into the structures of society.

- **We must watch as war is declared against an unseen, undefined enemy.** God's children will become warriors and embrace the difficult revelation of war. We will learn to war in the midst of glory (see Jude 20–25).

- **We need to watch as God gathers His scattered sheep.** A scattered people will be divinely returned. (This will help break the curse of scattering in your own life, from the Body of Christ and in the lands of the earth.) Watch as the Spirit of God rebuilds a broken-spirited Kingdom people who have been vexed by the enemy!

- **We must watch our emotions.** During changing times, emotions and anxieties erupt in our lives and environment, tossing us to and fro. The Spirit of the living God is hardening His people to circumstances. We will learn how to maintain a "cool spirit" in the midst of adversity.

- **We must watch David's Tabernacle manifest today.** God's people are transferring from a Word understanding to a glory demonstration. This will create the performance of God's glory. His will in heaven will now be seen and advance in the earth.

- **We must watch as new sounds create a new movement.**
  We must learn to hear the sound of triumph and march
  to the beat of victory.

- **We must watch the war of the sons of Greece vs. the
  sons of Zion.** As we watch, we must choose the "bever-
  age of war" that we wish to drink—water, oil or wine.
  In days ahead, we will war over the liquids of the earth.
  Most people think the war is over oil, but the real war,
  I believe, will be over water–though oil is an incredible, sustaining resource, one cannot live without water.
  Where the final battles of the world manifest, the first
  attacks of the enemy will be against the vineyards that
  produce wine for Shabbat. In every war, a certain bever-
  age will be key.

- **We must watch the rising war of provision.** Mammon, a god, will manifest in the rulers of the world.
  In this time, we must be on the lookout for the "evil
  eye," the deceptive ways of the enemy. We are called
  to see clearly, but Satan is always watching for that opportune time to vex and blind us from seeing the best
  that God has for us. He plans strategies to divert us
  from accomplishing God's will and entering into our
  heavenly Father's blessings. Many of us have a hard
  time *seeing* the enemy's snares strategically planted
  along our path, for the enemy likes to hide. The Bible
  explains that we can be blinded by his deceptive ways,
  but God gives us access to revelation that will uncover
  what has been kept secret (2 Corinthians 4:3–4, 6). We
  must unveil the evil eye and blind it instead of being
  blinded.

- **We must watch the choices of a maturing new generation.** How most of this generation—who have never

been in a declared war—views war in the natural and spiritual will be key to sustaining victory.

- **We must watch for our divine escape.** There is a way of escape, but not through escapism.

War Issues Will Soon Intensify

Are we awake and watching, or do we slumber? With the fall of the World Trade Center's Twin Towers in New York, the world was semi-awakened to the reality of a changing season of war. Warfare in the earth realm has done nothing but intensify since that moment. Following are some of the battlegrounds on which the present war will be fought.

1. **Manipulation of time and law.** Jesus came to earth at Father God's perfect timing. Jesus threatened the political and religious "machine," or system, by doing what Father said. This is one of the most important keys to victory.

   Daniel wrote of his vision, "The Ancient of Days came, and a judgment was made in favor of the saints of the Most High, and the time came for the saints to possess the kingdom" (Daniel 7:21–22). The Ancient of Days is going to favor us (the saints) in days ahead. Make no mistake, the time *will* come for the saints to possess the Kingdom. That means we *will* take domin-ion, govern, prevail and dominate the world powers around us. In verses 24 and 25, however, we find this:

   > The ten horns are ten kings who shall arise from this kingdom. And another shall rise after them; He shall be different from the first ones, and shall subdue three kings. He shall speak pompous words

against the Most High, shall persecute the saints of the Most High, and shall intend to change times and law. Then the saints shall be given into his hand for a time and times and half a time.

Notice what Scripture says the enemy does: He will attempt to change both *times and law*. There will be a great struggle in days ahead as Satan attempts to persecute the saints by getting us out of God's timing or controlling us so we cannot enter into God's timing. One of his tactics will be to change the laws around us. Many laws are already being developed to stop or constrict God's children from operating in freedom. This is why it is so critical for us to understand God's timing and the spiritual boundaries He has given us through His law, not the world's. If not, deception will easily enter into our lives.

2. **Root wars.** Generational iniquitous roots have formed thrones of iniquity that rule entire regions and nations. The root of iniquity goes back to the Garden and the Fall of man. Only through the redemptive blood of the Lord Jesus Christ can we overthrow that root and enter into all the spiritual blessings that He has for us in heavenly places (Ephesians 1:3).

3. **Trade iniquities.** (Joshua 13:3–5; 19:24–31; 2 Kings 19; Ezekiel 28; Revelation 19). Satan was thrown from heaven because of illegal trading practices. He longed to exalt those practices above the King of the universe. When he was cast from heaven, he used and continues to use sound to cover over wealth.

4. **The redemptive blood and glory of God.** We have to understand blood wars, for the Spirit of God will begin

to invade blood structures. Until God is ready to deal with the blood war in the land, there is no need to deal with it on your own. But when you pray, you can sometimes hear what the blood in the land is crying out. This allows you to become an advocate of reconciliation and deliverance.

5. **Worship.** Worship and sound have spiritual power. Worship is not just singing, but a form of communion, or giving, that realigns earth and heaven. Throw open your window and receive the sound of the Lord! Let the wind bring through your window the sound that you need. Your conscience is like a window between soul and spirit; make sure nothing is clouding your conscience. If we will cleanse our conscience, then the revelation that has not been available to influence our minds will find an entrance. This is the season of confession and decree; what we say now determines our future. Though the enemy is roaming like a mighty lion seeking to destroy, there is a roar in you to be released at this time. Open your mouth and release the shout of victory! This roar will defy the enemy. Go past that which seems invincible in your life. Get in the river of change that is flowing by your door and let it take you to your next place. Get a shield of protection around you and birth the new that the Lord has for you. Your end (future) will be greater than your beginning.

6. **Kingdom mysteries.** Jesus did much of His public teaching, especially teaching about the Kingdom, through parables. If we want to move forward with Him, we need to learn how to receive and respond to them. To walk in Kingdom authority, we must learn to decode parables and allow God to speak to us through them.

We might define a parable as a short, simple story designed to communicate a spiritual truth. It is not an allegory. An allegory is usually filled with symbolic meaning, and every detail means something. In contrast, parables generally have only one main point. Trying to overly symbolize a parable is usually unproductive. Parables are one form of the secrets or "mysteries" of God (see Matthew 13:11), which cannot be discerned by our physical senses. A mystery can only be known by revelation.

A parable *appears* to be understandable, but its true meaning cannot be discerned by just hearing the story. One needs a "key," a piece of information that interprets the parable. Only by receiving that key can the parable's meaning be understood. Many assume that Jesus spoke in parables to illustrate His messages, to make His teaching clear and understandable to everyone. Just the opposite is true. Jesus spoke in parables to conceal truth from some while revealing it to others (Mark 4:11–12). The multitudes heard His parables, but only His followers, whom He took aside privately, received the key.

Psalm 25:14 tells us, "The secret of the LORD is with those who fear Him, and He will show them His covenant." That is the point Jesus was making to His disciples in Matthew 13:11–13 (NIV):

> The knowledge of the secrets of the kingdom of heaven has been given to you, but not to them. Whoever has will be given more, and they will have an abundance. Whoever does not have, even what they have will be taken from them. This is why I speak to them in parables: "Though seeing, they do not see; though hearing, they do not hear or understand."

Those who willingly receive and respond to truth will always be given more, but those who reject it will be kept in ignorance. Why would God conceal truth from some? It is because of His mercy! Continuing to give revelation to those who resist God only increases their condemnation, so God, in His mercy, cloaked the truth in parables.

Another purpose of a parable is to bypass our defenses, allowing us to "hear the whole story." When the interpretation is given, our defenses are down, and then we are able to respond. We see this in the story of David and Nathan in 2 Samuel 12. God sent Nathan to David to confront David with his sin. If Nathan had spoken directly, David's defenses would have been up, and things would not have turned out well for Nathan. Instead, Nathan told a parable. When he heard about a rich man taking a poor man's sheep and killing it, David "caught" the picture and his emotions were aroused. Then all Nathan had to do was interpret the parable. The key was one simple phrase: "David, you are that man!" The full weight of David's sin suddenly hit him, and he repented.

7. **Healing and unusual workings of miracles.** Unusual miracles are going to start happening, as in Acts 5:15. Testimonies of healing give us faith, and when you get enough faith flowing, you are going to see unusual miracles. Some of you are "unusual miracle workers"—you will decree a thing, and it will happen while you are decreeing it. You may operate in the gift of miracles, but you have blocked, shut down and covered over that gift because of the religious paradigm of the Church and territory to which you belong. But we are not

fellowshiping the way we used to. The church that is built around fellowship simply will not have the same impact. These are war strategies. Unusual miracles will cause the atmosphere to go into war.

8. **Strategies of harvest.** We are going to define our fields, so that within the next few years we will plow and gather crops in new ways. Perversions that have held entire groups captive will start to break open. When this happens, we will need to look at homosexuals or those with AIDS in a different light. They are "harvest" groups. Keep in mind, though, that even harvest groups have an "ISIS contingency"—a relatively small faction willing to use militant and even violent means to advance a demonic agenda. This does not mean that all homosexuals are militant and ready to kill, any more than all Muslims align themselves with ISIS. God is going to deliver and set free many in these harvest groups. But, in the midst of His salvation, you are going to have to let Him destroy the tares among the wheat.

9. **Communication wars.** This age is marked by things that have never been seen in history. People have never been connected in the ways we are able to connect now. The demons are not new, but they have never had the tools to work with that they have now. Therefore, use wisdom in your communication wars. There is a war over communication, technology and media that is aligned in space through satellite systems. Cognitive processes and information access and retrievals are more advanced. This will produce great breakthroughs and great perversions.

10. **Border wars.** Borders are the edges that form the outer boundaries. The lines that separate countries, provinces, states, neighbors, landowners, etc., lead to conflicts. People groups war over borders.

11. **New paradigms for a new generation.** The emerging generation must begin to form new paradigms and create models for gatherings and gaining access to the throne of God. The question is whether these paradigms will be Word centered in this age. A dichotomy of good and evil is forming, bringing us into a season of polarization. We must understand God's covenant in these conflicts, for their root is anti-Semitic and controlled by mammon. We have to address the dichotomy of good and evil that is forming, because, I believe, the next generation *doesn't know what side they are on.* They have a concept that "good" is Church, but that is not what God is about. "Good" and "God" are two different worlds! God is good, but being "good" does not make us godly or enable us to fulfill the perfect will of God.

In the season ahead, our prayer lives will become more authoritative. What will happen once you pray is that the Holy Spirit will bring down certain judgments and start dealing with injustices. People entwined in their emotions with groups and situations that the Holy Spirit is addressing will either find a way of escape from the situation or be dealt with along with the corporate group. Do not be overmerciful and back down. Prayer works by faith, and faith works by love. You will then have to let God deal with the situation.

Upheavals and overturnings are part of the season ahead. You will simply have to say with confidence, *Lord, You sent me there to pray. I did. I will trust that You will work all this together for good, in both the tares and the wheat, and bring forth the harvest.*

Stay hidden in your abiding place, but also know when to come out. Know when to speak and when to be quiet. Prophesy! You war with your prophetic word. This is a prophecy for you to use in warring and watching; pray, decree and use this like a sword:

Watch carefully. Go where I send you. Do not go in your own strength, for it is I who is sending you forth. I am mobilizing you. I am giving you the strength to rise up. Go where I send you. Do not be frightened by what you hear. Do not back up just because giants seem near. Stand firm, for I am going before you. Just go with Me and say, "I have been sent to receive this blessing."

I can part what is unpartable. I can cause that which would not let go to now come apart so you can pass through. This is a time of showing. I plan on showing you what you are looking for. Do not back up, for the show is ready to begin! The show is ready to begin! Therefore, find your seat in Me and get ready to watch the manifestation that you have been asking Me about.

Your seat and your position have already been prepared for you. Come up! Through your worship, rise up and be seated with Me. Together we will decree into your atmosphere and change your condition. Come up, be seated and watch that area around you in the earth realm be filled with My presence. Come into a new place with Me. Join Me in a new way. I have blessings of which you know not that I long to pour out over you.

I have been looking for a group. I have been looking for the ones to anoint now. There is an anointing that I am bringing down from heaven so you can stand as one and break through the barrier that the enemy has erected. I am coming in now!

I am coming into your life in new ways. I am breaking that which has been around you. I am causing you to feel

My presence in new ways. I am causing you to be favored in new ways. I am breaking through the blood barrier in your brain. *You thought that knowledge could get through, but I have got to break that blood barrier where the iniquitous flow from prior generations continues to have the right to operate. I will cause you to come alive and see what I would see. I am breaking through a blood barrier! I am breaking through a blood barrier! What has been filed and cataloged is now coming alive. I am going to reverse some Alzheimer's. I am going to reverse some dementia. I am changing some things. I am going to reverse stuttering. I am going to reverse dyslexia. I am breaking through the blood barrier in your brain. My presence can penetrate.*

I will reveal My glory. I am coming to reveal so I can break open the seal that has closed up what you have been looking for. I am neutralizing your chromosomes from iniquitous patterns. Let My glory penetrate! Let My glory penetrate! I am breaking your insecurity barrier. I am uncovering the treasure that you have been. I am uprooting what has been buried deep and causing you to flower and blossom forth in a new way. *Let Me uproot! Let Me uproot!*

Prayer: *Father, You are going to start unlocking things in dreams and visions. You are going to start decoding revelations. Lead us back to pray one more time at certain places that have already been prayed at and where demons have been addressed. But this time, make the structure holding what is captive in a region to fall. Reveal the history and records of where others have gone before and how they have prayed. Let us find these portals to "bring down" and align heaven. Let us be known as the "tipping point" agent that tipped the bowl of incense into the earth!*

3

A New Mindskin for a New Wineskin

God's children must learn to war, but the key issue is whether they will develop a new way of thinking. If we are going to enter the war for harvest and triumph, we must think differently. I call this a "mindskin for God's new wineskin."

I didn't coin this phrase; Jerry Tuma, a well-known business leader, used it when we were teaching a business seminar. While he was addressing the changes occurring in the economic community and their effects on the Church, he said, "To meet these changes head-on, we must have a new *mindskin!*"[1]

Jerry meant to say "wineskin," but I immediately got up from my seat and shared that Jerry's slip of the tongue was really what a new wineskin is about—the way we think! We need to allow a shift in our thinking so we reflect the mind of God in the way we structure our ministries, businesses, families and lives. A new "mindskin" is the perfect picture for understanding what must happen for God's people to advance into a new way of expressing their identity.

A Kingdom wineskin understands the necessity of kingdom clashes. People with this "mindskin" know they must war for their inheritance. As a Kingdom people arising, we must not think like church attendees but like Kingdom warriors. We are the triumphant army of this age. We have access to revelation that the enemy cannot access. Father has been waiting to release this revelation to His children since before the ages began. How we access revelation and wisdom in this age and war with them will determine how our generations triumph.

Today, If You Will Hear My Voice

The Church is transitioning from one wineskin to another. Without transitioning we cannot receive revelation pertinent to this age. The prayer force of the Church must transition into a Kingdom understanding. We must pray in a "force" that creates Kingdom shifts. God's intercessors usually hear first because they have heeded the call to stand in the gap. In 2 Peter 1:12 we find, "For this reason I will not be negligent to remind you always of these things, though you know and are established in the present truth." The word *present* refers to the "now word" of the hour—expressing the manifold wisdom of God for this age.

Every pattern and example we need for overcoming is in the canonized Word of God. Even so, in this different age we need different methods for war. Our faith must not rest in the wisdom of men or women; rather we must be immersed in the power of God to win. The spirit of this world will not win this war. If we submit to the Holy Spirit—the only restrainer of evil in the earth realm, who searches our spirits to judge, convict and lead each to righteousness—then we will triumph.

We are called to combine spiritual truths with spiritual language that will confound the highest thoughts of those using the world's best wisdom. The spiritual man examines, investigates, inquires, questions and discerns all things. He is spiritually alive and has access to everything God is doing. The unspiritual man cannot receive the gifts necessary to ultimately overcome. The Church must be revived by the Spirit of God so that we become triumphant in the world. The Kingdom of God is not based on talk but on power.

All I am really doing is paraphrasing what Paul told the gifted, but relatively unsanctified, Corinthians. He revealed the ultimate goal of our Lord and Messiah as He works by His Spirit through us. An *end will come* when He, the Son, delivers the Kingdom to God the Father after nullifying and abolishing every other rule, authority and power. Christ must reign in the earth and put all of His enemies under His feet. His ultimate goal for the saints who die is that in Him they triumphed against their enemies, including death, and stood firm in their faith.

In 1 Corinthians 2:6–8, 10–12, Paul writes,

> We speak wisdom among those who are mature, yet not the wisdom of this age, nor of the rulers of this age, who are coming to nothing. But we speak the wisdom of God in a mystery, the hidden wisdom which God ordained before the ages for our glory, which none of the rulers of this age knew; for had they known, they would not have crucified the Lord of glory. . . . But God has revealed them to us through His Spirit. For the Spirit searches all things, yes, the deep things

of God. For what man knows the things of a man except the spirit of the man which is in him? Even so no one knows the things of God except the Spirit of God. Now we have received, not the spirit of the world, but the Spirit who is from God, that we might know the things that have been freely given to us by God.

This is the time for a new army of God to arise. This army, the triumphant reserve, does not just pray pastorally for the needs of those advancing but demonstrates an apostolic and prophetic authority. We are decreers and proclaimers. We must think differently! Ask the Lord to change your mind so you think like He thinks.

New Wine Is Pouring

The transition in the Body of Christ is really a changing of wineskins (see Mark 2:22). The new wine God longs to pour into His Body includes the power, understanding and wisdom that we will need to face the future war of the Church. Changing the wineskin—in this case a changing government in the Body—is a crucial part of our preparation for it. In his book *The Complete Wineskin*, Harold R. Eberle writes,

> Whenever the Holy Spirit fills people with "new wine," the structure or organization in which they function must change. Old wineskins rip. New wineskins must be used to hold the additional life and power of God. . . . The time for God to move is at hand. Therefore, we should expect our present wineskins to rip. . . . There can be no mighty spiritual awakening in our day without a great shaking of our Church organizations, leaders, and structures. If you are looking for the Second Coming of Jesus, or if you are praying to God to move upon your church, your city, your local schools, your

family, or your own heart, then the first thing you must look for is a new wineskin.[2]

The new wine only comes when it is time for God to give the Church revelation for how to be victorious in the next season. To do that, God has to restructure our wineskins in order to lay the foundations for future victory. Graham Cooke writes,

There is a new prototype of church emerging that will clash with the world and institutional Christianity. A prototype is the first in a series. The Church will rediscover her radical edge, but not by playing with the world's toys and using them differently. Real radical behavior in church is grounded in the supernatural. It proceeds from the mouth of God; it emanates from simple obedience to His ways; it emerges out of Holy Spirit boldness to follow the plans of God with fervent faith. It is to be willing to look foolish in order to confound the world.

We all will be pioneers in this next move of God. His plans for our churches will mean profound changes to the structure, vision, personality, and effectiveness of our meetings, missions, training, and discipleship forums. We will see a radical change in leadership style and methodology.

When building a prototype church, all our mistakes are public. One thing we should note here: Real pioneers do not criticize other pioneers because they know how hard it can be to build something new. Settlers usually make the most vicious of critics. They haven't done it themselves and have no intention of taking what they perceive to be insane risks. Their credo is that it is better to snipe from the sidelines and then borrow the new thing once it has been proved out. Some even argue that it is their "refining" comments that have played a valuable part in maturing the original concept.[3]

One Wineskin Prepares the Way for the Next

John the Baptist's ministry defined a certain wineskin. The only way people could get in it was through repentance. They came to the desert to see this move of God, repent (or, as John stated, change their minds from viperous ways) and be baptized. This wineskin created quite a stir! John and his disciples declared that the Kingdom of God was coming. They were preparing the way for Messiah to bring a baptism of fire.

John and his disciples had developed an order to paving the way. This place near the Jordan River would become "the place of the scapegoat." John preached repentance and turning from sins, using language like "vipers," "you snakes" and "Turn now!" As they named their sins in the wilderness, people were baptized. This was the way of salvation leading up to Jesus.

When Jesus of Nazareth, age thirty, left His home and occupation to align with this move, a major shift occurred. The time had come for John's wineskin to change into a structure that would exhibit a greater fullness. This changed history.

When John saw Jesus, he exclaimed that He did not really belong in this repentance movement. John knew who Jesus was and that the message of repentance from sin did not fit His character at all. The Lord simply stated that unless He aligned with the present move, He could not fulfill the righteous plan that Father had for Him. Jesus was then baptized, and what initiated Him to move forward into a greater plan was a direct atmospheric shift of heaven, with the voice of God commissioning Him for a new mission of redemption.

Each Baptism Is Important

Never negate the baptism of one move of God in hopes of jumping in on the next. That is not how a new wineskin operates. Jesus honored the wineskin of John and was immersed in the message of that wineskin. He took that baptism into the development of His wineskin.

After Jesus was initiated into ministry and spent forty days in the desert wilderness, He received a new baptism— not of water but of fire, a fire of heaven greater than any fire that hell could match. Having been led into the wilderness by the Spirit, He faced His adversary, who eventually withdrew. He went in one way and came out another, with power and authority to begin a new move of liberation, redemption and fulfillment. He faced off every temptation known to mankind. Thus His wineskin had a Kingdom power and force threaded through its structure that John's wineskin did not.

In Matthew 9:17, Jesus taught about the new move of God using an analogy of a wineskin. John's disciples and the Pharisees—the old wineskins—accused Him because His disciples did not exercise the spiritual discipline of fasting the way they did. Jesus essentially said, "We are not going to do it the old way, with the methods that worked in the past. You cannot put new wine in an old wineskin!" (see Matthew 9:17). In other words, a better-quality skin was needed to receive what God was going to pour out. Jesus said (my paraphrase), "If the new goes in the old, you will lose the old and the new. Let's preserve what has gotten us to this point. But let's also develop a new quality structure to hold the revelation that will be the fuel for us to advance."

Many Choose Not to Shift

Jesus then began forming *His* wineskin. Only Andrew, who came from John the Baptist's wineskin, made the shift to the new structure. In Matthew 11, John became disillusioned in prison and asked his disciples to find out if Jesus, the One he baptized, was really the One they were hoping for. In Matthew 14, John was beheaded. The new wineskin was forced to accelerate. By this time, John's disciples had either realigned with the Pharisees (see Matthew 9:14) or were seeking the new baptism.

Only Andrew left John in the wilderness and followed Jesus into the cities to eat with publicans and sinners. John was not excited about the changes that were coming to Israel through Jesus, the One for whom he had prayed, interceded and paved the way. To embrace a new wineskin, you must let go and quit clinging to the familiar. In fact, if you hold on to it, you will be limited in how you can grow, mature and efficiently operate in your place of stewardship. Here are some of the areas or old structures to which we cling:

- Our thought processes. We need a new mindskin.
- Old methods. Some are good, some are bad.
- Yesterday's message, which was great revelation but is not relevant today.
- A narrow form, one that was pliable in the past season but is now becoming rigid.
- Established markets. They released creative products for a time, but now new innovation is required.
- A great glory manifestation. This created belief and reorganized our lives, but now God is moving in a new way that is stretching us again.

- A lesser power and demonstration. He has more to show us.

The carnal mind is in enmity with God. You might ask, "How can the Church as a whole be carnal?" Old wineskins can refuse the methods and knowledge that God is bringing forth to reach the harvest. Usually the persecutor of the new wineskin is the old wineskin. Worship and sound are key for this shift, and we will discuss this more fully later. For now, you can refer to Cain and Abel in Genesis 4. Abel was murdered because Cain did not like God's acceptance of his firstfruits form of worship.

Both Must Choose to Advance

Jesus moved His disciples into a new season with His teaching and example. He raised a twelve-year-old girl from the dead. As He moved forward to reach this girl, a woman who had been ill with an issue of blood for twelve years pressed through the crowd to touch Him. He released His virtue, and she was immediately healed.

What can we learn from this? Time is significant, so look first at the twelve years. Twelve represents a new administration and the apostolic gift. The next generation, or administration (represented by the young girl), lay dormant, whereas the old administration (represented by the woman) was pressing through.

When Jesus determines to move into the new, we who are being taught by Him must choose to respond. The woman with the issue of blood had to press past the fact that she was a woman. She had to press past the law that barred anyone with an issue of blood from being out in public. There will always be a crowd that one must press through. But she was desperate, and the Lord acknowledged her and delivered her from her past season and its conflicting religious structure. As we press through and touch Him in our desperation, we begin our next season of new life.

Jarius' young daughter represented the next administration. When Jesus reached her, He said, "She is not dead, but sleeping" (Luke 8:52). When He commanded her to rise, the next administration awakened. The grief of one season must end in order for you to awaken to the next.

In this season we must go one way or the other. Choose the way to fullness! The Lord has a set time for causing a structure to shift, for He is sovereign over timing and change. The ruler of heaven, the King of kings, initiates these changes in the earth. Psalm 24:1 (KJV) says, "The earth is the LORD's, and the fullness thereof." He is the same yesterday, today and forever, so He knows when He is ready to take His Church into a new realm of understanding His goodness and love. He also knows the structure necessary to accommodate and produce His plan in the earth, saying, *I must enlarge you and that which I have given you to steward, so I can express Myself in new ways.*

A Holy Spirit–Empowered Peculiar People

If you are moving in the new, you will see several changes: His fullness will be seen in your personality. Your soul will be restored from the last season. All fear and manipulation that have crowded your identity and confined you to your past will leave your personality. Your new identity will reflect His ability to overcome the mountains that stopped your progress (see Isaiah 41 and Zechariah 4). He has given you power over your enemies that would hinder your progress (see 2 Corinthians 10:3–6).

We are a nation above all nations; concerning the governments of this world, however, we are called to pray for all those in authority, not just for those whom we prefer to win elections. We are a "peculiar people," not a political caucus. We can steer the course of history with our prayers and acts of faith. Jesus had to deal with the mindset of some of His key leadership who were more interested in making Him king of a nation than in recognizing Him as King of the Kingdom of God.

We must rely on the Holy Spirit as we enter a new season. He must become our rear guard as we advance. Unless the Holy Spirit is enfolded in the history of any land and continues directing its covenant with God, evil will overtake the society, causing the covenant root with our Creator to wither.

The Holy Spirit enables us to triumph as we go through great change. In approaching the future, the real issue always concerns the change of heart and unified expression of His people, since this will release an anointing throughout the earth. The anointing breaks the yoke (see Isaiah 10:27)! God always has a triumphant reserve from generation to generation that will come forth with new strength and power.

A Mindskin for the New Wine

Our mindskin produces God's wineskin for today and our future. Built on revelation, the Church advances the Kingdom of God in the earth. We have entered a new season in the history of the Church. Like each generation before us, we must have a structure relevant to expressing Jesus Christ, our Messiah, in this present age. The most critical issue is how we think. We express every structure of society based on our thought processes. Those who connect their thoughts with God's thoughts can change the history of the world in their age.

How we are thinking today does not just affect the belief system of our generation; it influences subsequent generations. I believe the most incredible challenge in the Body of Christ is to think the way the Lord thinks first, and then set our plans for the future. In the following chapters, we will look at some of the current trends in the Body of Christ and ask the Lord how we should respond in times like these.

The Church as a whole is undergoing a major transition, a Kingdom transition. Like the children of Issachar, we must understand the times in which we live so we can transition correctly (see 1 Chronicles 12:32). Scholars and watchers of Church trends agree that God is fashioning a new wineskin for His Church that will cause us to arise and take a stand against the kingdom of darkness. Let's take a look at how this new wineskin will appear in the days ahead.

A New Dawn Is Breaking

We have now entered into the third phase of a new war season. The first, I believe, was initiated during the uprising in Tiananmen Square in Beijing, China, in June 1989, when a single protester attempted to block the advance of tanks. This helped reveal China emerging as a prominent force in the earth. Related to this season was the United States and its allies going to war with Iraq in 1991. The second phase of war began when the United States and the world were shocked by the terrorist attacks of September 11, 2001. This revealed a war that was being initiated and would escalate until the end of time.

We need a new anointing to break open God's full purposes. At the breaking of each new season, we must renew our commitment to the One who made us and gives us life. Psalm 37:5–6 (TLB) says, "Commit everything you do to the Lord. Trust him to help you do it, and he will. Your innocence will be clear to everyone. He will vindicate you with the blazing light of justice shining down as from the noonday sun." The word *new* is defined as "different from one of the same which existed before; or made fresh."

New seasons bring new relationships. May your relationship with the Lord be new and fresh, and may He supernaturally connect you horizontally with others who will cause you to come into a greater level of success. New acts will occur in your life with signs, wonders and miracles. We as believers will actually be known for our new identity. The Lord is making His children whole to reflect Him. His fullness will flow through your personality, and a new garment of favor will be worn with your new identity. You will radiate with favor and enter into new opportunities.

We must suit up in the armor for today and use new weapons for the war ahead. The trumpet is sounding a new sound; listen carefully. New sounds accompany His new army. May you receive everything you need to defeat your enemies. May you hear the sound of victory and shout this sound from the rooftops. May you be anointed in a way that every yoke is broken. May you receive the ability to stand in dominion in the sphere of authority that you have been granted by God. We all should be looking for the Lord to reveal these things to us in a *kairos* time in the earth.

From Church to Kingdom

From generation to generation and season to season, the Lord rebuilds His Church so His Kingdom can be better manifested in the earth. Therefore, we must understand the

Kingdom of God. Later we will discuss a structure God is presently reestablishing in the Church called apostolic centers. Apostolic centers reflect His Kingdom manifested on earth as it is in heaven.

Shifting Into the Kingdom

Earlier we reviewed how Jesus formed His new wineskin. He does not, however, really express the understanding of Kingdom until Matthew 11, when John questioned Him from prison. John sent his disciples to ask, "Are You the Coming One, or do we look for another?" Jesus answered, "The blind see and the lame walk; the lepers are cleansed and the deaf hear; the dead are raised up and the poor have the gospel preached to them" (Matthew 11:3, 5). Jesus was saying, "Go tell John that I'm doing everything he prophesied would be done." Then He added, *"Blessed is he who is not offended because of Me"* (verse 6).

That should be a warning to us. To paraphrase Jesus, "If your disciples don't get offended by the way I am doing things in this new administration, they can move forward into the new. But they must choose not to get offended." The passage continues:

> As they departed, Jesus began to say to the multitudes concerning John: "What did you go out into the wilderness to see . . . a prophet? Yes, I say to you, and more than a prophet. For this is he of whom it is written: 'Behold, I send My messenger before Your face, who will prepare Your way before You.' Assuredly, I say to you, among those born of women there has not risen one greater than John the Baptist; but he who is least in the kingdom of heaven is greater than he."
>
> Verses 7, 9–11

In other words, up until that moment, there had not been a greater man than John; but God's people were moving from a season of paving the way into forming a new administration. As they moved into the new, those transitioning into Kingdom life would be greater than that which was previously experienced and modeled by John. That was a big shift!

Jesus continued, "From the days of John the Baptist until now the kingdom of heaven suffers violence, and the violent take it by force. For all the prophets and the law prophesied until John" (verses 12–13). In other words, all the prophets prophesied up until that point. The Law ruled up to this moment in history, but something was about to shift. This explains what they were seeing in the new administration. Everything they had experienced until that time had been good and necessary, but now things were going to shift. They needed to see and understand the shift. Essentially, Jesus was telling John that He was fulfilling all the things that had been prophesied. If one is not offended, one can *see* prophecy being fulfilled. Offense blinds us to what is happening in the Kingdom.

The Difference between Kingdom and Church

We need to understand the difference between Kingdom and Church. The Kingdom is the whole of God's redeeming activity in Christ in the world. He oversees and reviews what Kingdom strategies of His are manifesting in the seven-mountain structure of society. The Church is the assembly of those who belong to Christ Jesus. Dutch Sheets puts it this way: "Kingdom takes visible form in those who have assembled as the Church." As we make this shift in our understanding, we will start manifesting the Kingdom. When we assemble, we should have a much greater power than that which we exhibit alone. We need to ask God to shift us into a greater holy array so that He can come and meet us in a new way.

Kingdom people are sent out to do Kingdom work. As Kingdom representatives advance, they will meet opposing forces. Kingdom people know warfare and do not back off from it. They know that kingdoms are in conflict and have learned to maneuver in the warfare of the Kingdom. They are not trying to protect themselves. They are on a mission every time they leave their front doors. We have been given grace and faith to overcome the antichrist forces.

The Spirit of God is now developing centers where a Kingdom display can occur. The Lord not only declares His Word, He performs His Word and manifests His glory. These apostolic centers are prototypes of heaven for all the earth to see.

In *The Apostolic Church Arising*, a recent book Robert Heidler and I wrote together, we explain the characteristics of the Kingdom, which many do not understand. Often people relate the concept of kingdom to worldly structures, but that is not the highest level of Kingdom rule. When you begin with the way God set up His Kingdom, the world will not be able to conform you to a lower expression of kingdom. Here are the characteristics of a Kingdom-minded entity advancing in the earth[4]:

- **Kingdom has a government.** We see the importance of government in the Kingdom in the Jesus Movement of the 1960s. God brought multitudes into His Kingdom, but there was no government in place to secure the harvest. Though many came in, much of that harvest was lost. Kingdom must have a supernatural government: We must understand Lord Sabaoth, the Lord of

Hosts. We must understand how Jehovah-Nissi sends His government into war.

- **Kingdom is ruled by a king.** We must not forget that our King has sovereign rule over His government. He can promote you or sit you on a shelf for a year. We submit to earthly rulers, but when we understand all authority structures, we can maneuver in them as representatives of the Kingdom of God.

- **Kingdom has administration.** Kingdom administration is different from the church administration to which we have been accustomed. Administration can be difficult to grasp, but it is vital: To come into all that God wants, we must understand the Church's role in the Kingdom. You cannot express Kingdom by doing as Israel did at the end of the book of Judges, when all the people "did what was right in their own eyes." People who refuse to discover their places or positions in a new season cannot operate in the ultimate Kingdom expression God desires for them.

- **Kingdom has a culture.** If we conform to the cultures around us and never learn Kingdom culture, we will fail. We have lived at a lower level than what God wants for us because we have not expressed the culture of the Kingdom. Kingdom culture is higher than those of the world.

- **Kingdom is good news.** Kingdom is an alignment with the One who is giving us access from the throne. He who died for us and overcame all powers and principalities is now mediating for us to display His authority in the earth. This is good news for the world. If we do not demonstrate God's rule in the earth realm, we are not being the ambassadors God is calling us to be. Because

Kingdom requires a corporate response, our gifts must align and be ordered before certain demonic forces can be overcome.

- **Kingdom is connected through generations.** Though the Kingdom of God is within us, God is a tri-generational God. For a new generation to arise successfully, they must understand the history from where they have come and connect to the generations that come before and after. In our culture, young people are usually focused on establishing their own lives; the danger is that they can miss Kingdom authority. One of the cries of my heart is for the next generation to grasp the meaning of Kingdom.

- **God's heavenly Kingdom is not based on worldly patterns.** This causes some people to be confused about salvation. I think more people are saved than we realize, but not all of them enter into Kingdom. A heart for God does not equal expressing Kingdom in the earth. If you do not understand Kingdom, you become judgmental and critical as you see people striving to work out their salvation.

- **God's Kingdom is beyond man's natural thoughts.** The Bible says that the Kingdom cannot be comprehended by the natural mind. You have to get Kingdom from a supernatural dimension; it must be revealed. Ask the Lord to bring you into a higher level of Kingdom understanding.

- **Kingdom cannot be obtained by ambition.** Remember when the "Sons of Thunder" tried to do just that? Even their mother was ambitious. This is not a good thing. Nor is it when wives or husbands try to force a spouse into a more spiritual place. Ambition is a mean demon. This is what Judas had; he was ambitious for the Kingdom, but his ambition shifted him out of the eternal structure that he had been offered and into a role that led to destruction.

- **Kingdom should never be postponed.** When God is ready, He will move. The culture shock of moving between kingdoms can get you in a mess, however. We have to ask the Lord to keep us abreast of the way He is moving and learn how to represent Kingdom properly.

- **Kingdom has provision.** Kingdom supply structures will be one of the greatest changes we see in this shift, and we must understand them. We have garments and mantles that dress us, for we put on Christ daily.

- **Kingdom has a territory.** To establish the Kingdom in any territory, you must first develop the presence of God. This is why David's kingdom, which operated around the Ark of the Covenant, came closest to reflecting the pattern of heaven. God's presence was established in the Tabernacle of David because God was enthroned on the praises of Israel. If you put Church above Kingdom, you will develop the "gathering" structure as your priority rather than the "presence" structure. You will not be driven by God's presence; instead you will end up program driven to meet the needs of the people. Eventually, the people will still have to move into the presence of God to succeed.

- **Kingdom has an atmosphere.** Unless God's presence is established, you will not move forward. Beginning with God's presence is more difficult, because it cannot be understood from the world's perspective. The world understands gathering to meet people's needs. A church can look not much different from the world—gathering for fellowship, enjoying each other and meeting people. But if you are presence driven, meeting needs is not a driving motivation. This is the key to the seven mountains of human society; we move from God's Kingdom into the structures of the world.

- **Kingdom has prophets.** God ordains people who represent Him in every aspect of His authority. David had recorders and scribes, and so do I. At our ministry, Glory of Zion, they record everything we do, as well as significant dreams, because I value God's word and its expression.

- **Kingdom has war units.** God's Kingdom people war against demonic forces. This is the difference between Kingdom and our traditional concept of church. You can "go to church" without ever going to war, and you can have great fellowship with people but never war with them. At Glory of Zion, we have war units who will gather for intercession at 3:00 a.m. if God calls us to war during that watch. This is a military unit meeting with God to gain strategy to overcome the enemy.

- **Kingdom has gatekeepers.** Some gatekeepers can be challenging. I have had gatekeepers check my name tag before letting me into a conference! But this is the function of gatekeepers: They question who is coming in and out of the gate. In this way they fulfill what Jesus prophesied in Matthew 16 about the gates of hell by binding, forbidding or permitting. This is how we exercise authority when the Lord is executing His Kingdom plans in the earth.

- **Kingdom has treasurers.** The greatest warfare is in the treasury; therefore we establish those who can serve as treasurers. They have to understand and be accountable for key information and resources.

- **Kingdom has music and sound.** I love "free for all" dance, but at times the dance has to represent an order. If you have expressive corporate dance, it must be interpreted just like tongues. If sound and dance are not interpreted, then there is something lacking in Kingdom demonstration.

- **Kingdom has people who serve as the priests and Levites did.** The sanctuary would not be cared for were it not for the Levites. At Glory of Zion, we have one of the most incredible Levitical structures in the world. If it did not function so efficiently, we could not do what we do. Recently, one of our retired widows dusted everything in the sanctuary. God notices this and makes sure the Levites are cared for properly. You do not have to worry about being taken care of in Kingdom rule.

- **Kingdom has chief ministers.** I am extremely thankful for the chief ministers God has established at Glory of Zion, who minister and help others minister. They have gone through much and have testimonies of overcoming.

- **Kingdom has power.** A new power and anointing is being infused from heaven into those representing the Kingdom in earth. This power produces demonstration and causes a manifestation of glory.

We are moving into a new Kingdom age—this is a time to shift!

4

Why Christians Must Learn War

Learning war comes easier to some than others. To those who grew up in relative peace and comfort, it may come hardest of all. Why war? Why is war necessary? Why can people not live in harmony? These are the questions we ask our parents when we are first exposed to conflict through the media. We ask our history teachers when we are learning the events that brought us to the present. Most importantly, we ask God. "If You are a loving God," we question, "why do war and destruction occur?"

The short answer is that we are called to serve in God's army of warriors. If we do not heed His call, then the enemy will step in, and he will rule in our stead. We are called to possess, secure and protect our inheritance.

For Christians, war is not an easily understood dynamic of spiritual life. But understanding God's call to war is so important that it was worth devoting an entire chapter to explaining it. As I did for ten years in a master's/doctoral course at Southwestern College (now Southwestern Christian University), I will attempt to teach the spiritual dynamics of the training God's children endure to become warriors.

Should Christians Embrace War?

War is a fact of history, but for God's people—whether in biblical times or now securing the inheritances of His promises—war is difficult. At times, we must war to prosper. War then becomes dynamic through which revelation is communicated to mankind on how to live a godly life. Fortunately, the Bible is not just a history book but a book of life principles that shows us how to prosper, in war as much as in peace.

Peter C. Craigie, in his book *The Problem of War in the Old Testament*, describes three distinct problems that Christians have with the biblical concept of war:

1. **The problem of God.** That He is a warrior is a dimension of His character.
2. **The problem of revelation.** God reveals times when we must war.
3. **The problem of ethics.** The Ten Commandments— the basis of most legal justice systems—define times to pursue conflict and war that result in killing and death.[1]

A great gap of understanding seems to cause modern Christians to not fully embrace the Old Testament. Yes, Christianity was birthed in the New Covenant; faith, however, was initiated at the beginning of God's intervention in the earth. The Old Testament was the Bible of the New

Testament believers. In both covenants, then, we find the truth of war both physically and spiritually.

To profit from reading the Old Testament, we must have an overall perspective and intelligent response to deal with war. War can occur from natural as well as man-made circumstances, and both examples are included in the Old Testament. Most of us believe the New Covenant requires us to turn the other cheek. Jesus, however, said He came to bring not peace but a sword. We will always have to take a stand on what we believe. During New Testament times is when Christians were martyred!

In young people, I find the Old Testament is the major influence on their attitudes toward the Bible. Most children growing up in developed societies are taught Bible stories, and most of these are about war and overcoming—David and Goliath probably being the most popular! A young boy took on a giant and overcame him through the empowerment of the God of heaven. Jesus demonstrated the same incredible slaying of a giant by enduring the warfare of the wilderness and the cross to free mankind from bondage. We never want to hamper one's ability to see a giant and have faith to fell him with one stone. Without understanding the concept of war presented in the Old Testament, the next generation will have no idea how to combat the evils of the world.

Wars are usually a turning point in the history of nations, affecting entire cultures and generations. War can also determine the rise and fall of bloodlines, people groups and the ruling influences of the world. Great responsibility must be taken when dealing with warfare, whether physical, national or spiritual. We should never negate our legacy of war. "The LORD is a man of war" (Exodus 15:3). When He led the people out of Egypt and through the Red Sea, He revealed a new dimension of who He was: Jehovah-Nissi became a reality not only to the Israelites but to the entire region. God as warrior provides hope to all mankind. At the same time, we are required to embrace the Lamb, whose ultimate goal is peace.

The key to warfare is understanding the Kingdom, for war is about kingdoms in conflict. To withstand the world's confusion and conflicts on the horizon, we must get a strong, stable understanding of warfare, both physical and spiritual. In *God's Unfolding Battle Plan: A Field Manual for Advancing the Kingdom of God*, I write about several wars that are necessary to understand for God's children to walk in victory and fullness: wars over the mind, time, God's presence and glory, power, wealth, the nations and blood.

Of these, the blood war is the most important for our understanding of warfare. Blood joined God and humanity. Within the blood can lie the warfare of past iniquities as well as the redemption that unlocks eternity. Your blood wars for and against your destiny. Once His Spirit comes into your bloodline, all iniquities hidden in your DNA can be exposed.

People groups are really blood groups, which propel the ideologies of our minds and produce the lusts and ambitions that create wars. Only by allowing the Spirit of God to enlighten our spirits and flow through our blood can we triumph against the warfare of iniquity.

The Laws of War and the Prohibition of Murder

The book of Deuteronomy, which rehashes the history of Israel at their point of entry into their future, contains an exegesis of ancient customs and laws. This is not a corpus of law but a historical record of it. In its midst we find the history of warfare in the wilderness. We also find God giving laws for war in the Promised Land in chapter 20.

When the Lord calls us to war, He gives us the grace to triumph. God never calls His children to do anything without releasing the grace necessary to fulfill His purpose. Therefore, in the midst of war, there is grace to fight.

Theory of war is not the same as the practice of war. The laws of war should never be executed without the love of God. We should have an intense love of mankind and a need to see justice brought forth that justify using these laws to accomplish the purposes of those God calls to be His reconcilers. (As they contested the land, for example, God Himself asked Israel to offer a covenant alignment with the enemies in their path; if they refused to submit, only then did He allow His people to go to war.) God longs for His glory and presence to invade, and only those who carry His glory and presence can be used in reconciling heaven and earth. Sometimes war is necessary, even though the byproducts of war—fear, death and destruction—cause us to resist even the concept of it. Yet without the shedding of blood, sometimes we never see justice.

The results of death in war are not the same as the prohibition of murder. Death occurs in war. Murder, however, is a premeditated sin against life. The prohibition of murder, which can be found in most cultures, resulted from God's Law. War, on the other hand, is a manifestation of God's character against injustice. There are times when we must go to war!

The confusion of war with murder by most Christians who oppose warfare is embodied in the movie *Sergeant York*, about a real warrior of WWI named Alvin York. York is a poor, young Tennessee hillbilly who left a life of violence and licentiousness after experiencing a religious awakening at a revival. When the United States declares war, he tries to avoid conscription into the Army as a conscientious objector, for he does not believe in fighting due to his religious beliefs. He is drafted nonetheless.

York's sympathetic commanding officer tries to convince him of the need to make a sacrifice for his country and allows him a leave to think it over. While York is fasting and pondering, the wind blows his Bible open to the verse, "Render therefore unto Caesar the things which are Caesar's; and unto God the things that are God's." York reports again for duty and agrees to serve, leaving the matter in God's hands.

In the Meuse-Argonne Offensive of October 1918, York and his unit find themselves pinned by deadly machine gun fire. As he sees his comrades shot down, York's self-doubt disappears. He works his way to a position flanking the main enemy trench and shoots with such devastating effect that the Germans surrender. York and the handful of survivors take control of 132 prisoners.

York is awarded the Medal of Honor and explains his actions by saying that he was trying to save the lives of his men. He refuses opportunities to commercialize his fame, saying he is not proud of what he did in the war, but that it had to be done.

Not Peace but a Sword

No one went through more warfare and violence than Jesus of Nazareth. Once He set His face like a flint (see Luke 9:51) to accomplish His mission, He experienced the greatest of all conflicts. He was accused, abused and physically accosted—then He taught us to walk like Him. He even says in Luke 14:31 to consider the cost when going to war.

In Matthew 10:34 the Lord said, "Do not think that I came to bring peace on earth. I did not come to bring peace but a sword." Peace means wholeness or completeness. Sometimes the only way wholeness and completeness can manifest is through war. One of Jesus' purposes was to divide asunder the soul and spirit in individuals, families and territories. He cut away all dross that would cause decay, in order to eventually cause heaven's will to manifest.

We often forget that Jesus was the full expression of Father God. God is a warrior; therefore, when Jesus came, He was a warrior. He confronted the Pharisees and Sadducees. He rendered to Caesar what was Caesar's, but He never bowed His knee to Rome. He expressed force against injustice. He lived in warfare to show us how to confront both spiritual and physical entities. No matter how He addressed the enemies of His mission, His love was perfect. That is why He ultimately triumphed. His warfare was an expression of God's glory.

War is in the New Testament just as in the Old. The same warfare concepts are found in both, and they are not just applicable physically but spiritually. Like Jesus, thousands of martyrs under both covenants have given their lives for our faith, and they overcame.

A Surprising Introduction to War

To help us understand spiritual warfare, I want to reveal it in a surprising place: the Christmas story! Most Christians cannot reconcile warfare from Old to New Covenant; they see the Old Testament as literal war, but when they get to the New Testament—despite the cross and persecution that produced the Church—they think peace and grace. The Christmas story can help reconcile the need for our role in warfare.

Christmas can be controversial for Christians and Jews and emotionally stressful for all—even those who do not know Christ. Most scholars have determined, however, that Christ wasn't born in this season but at the Feast of Tabernacles in the fall. Consequently, one can surmise that the *conception* of Jesus occurred during what we think of as Christmastime. The Spirit hovered over a young virgin during the time that we celebrate His birth. He "invaded" darkness to defeat it, and His timing was perfect!

Several years back, when Robert Heidler and I were developing the Issachar School to teach prophetic people to understand time, we studied Matthew 1:17: "So all the generations from Abraham to David are fourteen generations, from David until the captivity in Babylon are fourteen generations, and from the captivity in Babylon until the Christ are fourteen generations." Jesus did not come randomly. A fullness of captivity in the earth had manifested, and three cycles of fourteen meant that the time for the Deliverer had come! A portal opened from earth to heaven, and Father God sent His best gift to redeem mankind. We need to celebrate "more of Christ" in *Christmas*—the *Mashach*, the Anointed One—so that each year we overcome evil's strategies in the world.

Though Matthew and Luke give detailed accounts of Jesus' birth, John sums up the story in one brief line: "The Word became flesh and dwelt [literally 'tabernacled'] among us, and we beheld His glory" (John 1:14). To those who understand it, that verse is incredible. But John 1:5 sums up Jesus' coming even more briefly: "The light shines in the darkness, and the darkness did not overcome it." That is Christmas! It is about light invading darkness, about Jesus, eternal King of the universe, bringing a light that cannot be overcome.

As I write this, we are in the Hebrew year 5776. Hebrew, our covenant language, helps us understand time so we know what to do. The Hebrew letter *vav* is the sixth letter in the alphabet, and it is associated with each year in a decade ending in six. *Vav* was originally a picture of a connecting pin or tent peg, which is still what the letter looks like. In the Hebrew language, *vav* is used for the word *and*; it joins seasons, cycles, individuals and things. It appears first in Genesis 1:1: "In the beginning God created the heavens *vav* the earth"—so the first *vav* in the Bible is used to connect the heavens and the earth. The Spirit hovered over the earth so the voice of God from heaven could *vav* the chaos and create new order.

At God's decree, "Let there be light," the Jews picture a single beam of light from God's infinite source shining into the universe. *Vav* is a picture of that beam of light. It is heaven invading earth, light illuminating darkness. We celebrate this very thing at Christmas—an invasion of earth by the light of heaven.

A Tale of Two Kingdoms

As I said earlier, war is about kingdoms in conflict. The Bible is the history of two kingdoms. The Kingdom of God is the Kingdom of light, eternal in the heavens. It is often symbolized in the Bible as a mighty mountain. The other kingdom is a counterfeit kingdom, the kingdom of darkness ruled by an evil tyrant, Satan; the bad news is that we live in Satan's territory. These two kingdoms are locked in conflict. If we want to understand the Bible, it is important that we understand these kingdoms. (That is the other reason to understand the power of the Christmas story: Jesus came to destroy the works of the devil, the evil one; see 1 John 3:8.)

God's Kingdom is an authority structure in the heavenly realms; on its throne is Jesus, the true King of the Universe. From there He rules over all creation. His government is carried out by rank after rank of angelic beings. But on earth the Kingdom of God is found within us.

Unfortunately, God's Kingdom is not the only government with power. In Isaiah 14, we see Lucifer, the angel assigned to lead all of creation in worship, becoming puffed up with pride and deciding to take God's glory for himself. Verses 12–14 describe his rebellion:

> How you are fallen from heaven, O Lucifer. . . . For you have said in your heart: "I will ascend into heaven, I will exalt my throne above the stars of God; I will also sit on the mount of the congregation on the farthest sides of the north; I will ascend above the heights of the clouds, I will be like the Most High."

Satan led a third of the angels in his doomed rebellion, and he and his followers were cast out of heaven. When Satan was cast down, he set up a counterfeit kingdom and put himself at the top.

In the Garden of Eden, when Adam submitted to Satan, the dominion God had given to Adam transferred to Satan. That is why the New Testament tells us that "the whole world lies under the power of the evil one" (1 John 5:19 NRSV). Satan is now the "god of this world" (2 Corinthians 4:4 KJV), which is why we have suffering, sickness and death. We are living in enemy territory.

94

You can tell what the kingdom of darkness is like by look-ing at its founder. Isaiah 14 tells us that Satan became puffed up with pride, expressed in five "I will" statements:

- *I will* ascend into heaven.
- *I will* exalt my throne above stars of God.
- *I will* sit on the mount of the congregation on the sides of the north.
- *I will* ascend above the heights of the clouds.
- *I will* be like the Most High.

Satan's pride led to ambition and self-exaltation. (He de-termined to *ascend* into heaven and *exalt* his throne.) His goal was to usurp authority. (He determined to sit on the mount of the congregation, which symbolizes authority and government.) He also made it his goal to take God's *glory* (the clouds being a picture of the clouds of glory that surround God's throne) and to seize God's place for himself. Satan's rebellion resulted in the release of God's judgment. He had tried to exalt himself but instead was brought down to the lowest depths of the pit (see Isaiah 14:15).

Satan's rebellion reveals the operating system of his king-dom, and it is what holds the world in darkness. The kingdom of darkness is based on pride, ambition, self-exaltation, a desire to usurp authority, a desire to receive glory and a de-sire to take the place of God. Wherever you see those things, Satan's kingdom is being manifested. No wonder our world has such a history of war, oppression and suffering!

Jesus invaded the darkness by using a different operating system, as we see in Philippians 2:6–10 (NASB):

Although He existed in the form of God, he did not re-gard equality with God a thing to be grasped, but emptied

Himself, taking the form of a bond-servant, and being made in the likeness of men. Being found in appearance as a man, He humbled Himself by becoming obedient to the point of death, even death on a cross. For this reason also, God highly exalted Him, and bestowed on Him the name which is above every name, so that at the name of Jesus every knee will bow.

Jesus' operating system was exactly the opposite of Satan's. Jesus introduced a different system based on humility, not seeking His own glory, emptying Himself and taking the form of a servant and submitting to the Father . . . even to the point of death.

Whose Side Are You On?

Ask any soldier what matters most on the battlefield, and you will likely get a two-fold answer. First, it is crucial to know whose side you are on. Who enlisted you? Who trained you for war? Whose tactics do you adhere to, and whose commands will you follow to the death?

As Christians, we are warriors who have been called and enlisted by the Holy God of this universe. His Spirit is the only force that will overcome the enemy; the Holy Spirit is the only restrainer of evil in the earth realm. The people of God must embrace and be empowered by His Spirit. We then become the enforcers and restrainers of evil in the earth.

We are warriors representing His Spirit. In the heat of battle, we must remind ourselves of the truths about the God who enlisted us. He is God above all gods. His Son has paid the price for our ultimate victory. Satan's headship has already been broken by the power of the cross; Jesus has already conquered death, hell and the grave. We need not fear death but only resist its sting. The Spirit of God reigns supreme in the earth to comfort us in the midst of distressing times. He gives us strategies to overcome every plot the enemy has set against our lives. The earth belongs to God, and He has a plan linked with the fullness of time. We, His children, might get knocked down, but we will never get knocked out. He is love, and perfect love in us will cast out all fear of the future.

With everything going on in the earth, we must never forget that He is God. We know that He is always in command. Yet if that is the case, why is there so much confusion around us? Why are nations in conflict and people groups warring against each other? Why does lawlessness continue to escalate? If He is God and has already won the victory, what exactly is our role in the midst of daily warfare?

The truth is that we are fully engaged in a covenant conflict, which means that we are warring to see the blessings of a holy, supreme God spread throughout the earthly realm. Psalm 24:1 (KJV) declares that "the earth is the LORD's, and the fulness thereof." God has a plan of fullness for the earth. His desire is for wholeness. Yet the war between God and evil is unfolding, and this determines how His fullness will be manifested in the earth in our generations and those to come.

Know Your Enemy

These are crucial times. We must know whose side we are on. The other crucial element to warfare is knowing *who you are fighting against*. Paul answers this question in Ephesians 6:12: "For we do not wrestle against flesh and blood, but against principalities, against powers, against the rulers of the darkness of this age, against spiritual hosts of wickedness in the heavenly places." Our war is and will continue to be with

1. Satan (Genesis 3:15; John 8:44; 2 Corinthians 2:11; James 4:7; 1 Peter 5:8; 1 John 3:8; Revelation 12:17)
2. The flesh (Romans 7:23; 1 Corinthians 9:25–27; 2 Corinthians 12:7; Galatians 5:17; 1 Peter 2:11)
3. Those who delight in evil (Psalm 38:19; 56:2; 59:3)
4. The world (John 16:33; 1 John 5:4–5)
5. Death (1 Corinthians 15:26; Hebrews 2:14–15)

Most wars are a result of the lust for power in mankind, causing conflict and calamity. Such wars are rooted in a three-stranded cord of religion, poverty and infirmity, creating barrenness instead of fullness in the earth.

We already know that the headship of Satan has been broken forever. He was defeated the moment Christ went to the cross, gave His life and shed His blood. When He rose from the dead, Jesus conquered death, our last enemy. Ultimately, we are fighting a war in which we are destined for victory. We must contend, however, with the worldly powers, principalities and dominions that continue to withhold the manifest blessings of "this age."

Satan may be defeated, but he is certainly still attempting to rule. Each generation is called to enforce on the earth the power of the cross and the resurrection. Satan and his hordes only have dominion when we negate the authority Christ has given us. As Christ's representatives on this earth, it is our calling to see His victory through. And that means war!

Satan rules demons, powers, principalities and a host of dark evil forces. John Eckhardt, in *Fasting for Breakthrough and Deliverance*, says that some demons

> are stronger, more wicked, unclean, and stubborn, and higher in rank, ability, and intelligence. The longer a demon has

been in your family or in your life, the harder it is to remove because its roots go very deep. Demons such as rebellion, pride, witchcraft, Jezebel, poverty and lack may only come out with a high level of faith. Sometimes it seems as if they cannot be dislodged, and people will get discouraged and frustrated and feel they have failed. . . . Sometimes you have to do something unusual, extraordinary and beyond the norm to see breakthrough. Normal church, normal Christianity, normal preaching, and normal praying are not going to get the job done. Some little, sweet prayer is not going to do. Religion won't get it done. It is going to take an anointing that destroys the yoke.[2]

We will discuss in depth triumphing and overcoming in other chapters. Just remember that today Satan still attempts to build his throne of iniquity and direct all worship, homage and resources of man to himself.

Exposing the Antichrist System

We are called to expose the works of darkness in the earth. I wrote extensively about the antichrist system in *The Future War of the Church*, and I highly recommend reading it for deeper understanding of this end time opposition. For now, I will summarize some of the main points. By "antichrist system" I am not referring to the person of the Antichrist. Rather, the antichrist system is the demonic structure that holds as its main mission destruction of the Body of Christ. Whether those involved in this system are aware or not, it is established to directly attack the Church and prevent her from advancing the Kingdom of God. (For more insight, read 1 and 2 John.)

In counseling God's children I have found that many are unaware about who really is opposing them. Many are going through horrid trials but never pause to find the source of the confusion. One businessman that I was counseling recently was sharing how God was leading him through a vision and how he was pursuing prosperity. He seemed to be blocked in the breakthrough, however. I finally said, "Now, tell me what the devil and his hordes are doing in your life." He looked at me in astonishment and replied, "That thought never entered my mind!" Once he had identified the enemy's strategy in his life, he was increasing within weeks.

> Let no one deceive you by any means; for that Day will not come unless the falling away comes first, and the man of sin is revealed, the son of perdition, who opposes and exalts himself above all that is called God or that is worshiped, so that he sits as God in the temple of God, showing himself that he is God.
>
> 2 Thessalonians 2:3–4

The antichrist system can manifest and be driven by politics or any form of religion. Jesus instructed us to take heed and beware of the leaven of the Pharisees, Sadducees and Herod (see Matthew 16:11 and Mark 8:15). These show how systems combine religious and political agendas to withstand God's plan on earth. The Antichrist used these structures to attack the One the Father sent to the world to redeem us. Their motivations crucified the Lord. All of them oppose the Good News that came to redeem and free those captivated by sin, as well as those representing the Kingdom of God (in the person and mission of Jesus Christ). Two clear modern-day examples of the antichrist system are Nazism and Communism, which have seen their rise and fall, yet still linger in our world. We also see it prevalently in the form of ISIS and Boko Haram, which means "Western education is forbidden."

The antichrist system can be defined by five distinct operations, each of which has been used to create a lack of blessing within the Church's domain. An explanation of each follows.[3] As I stated in *The Future War of the Church*,

> Satan knows full well that the blessings of God cannot rest on a region that is controlled by any of these. The Church, therefore, is going to have to develop a strategy to gain victory over these things in the days ahead if we are to make progress in winning the war for souls.[4]

1. **Anti-Semitism.** At the core of the antichrist spirit is a spirit of anti-Semitism, which creates division—a baseless hatred—between the Jewish people, God's covenant nation, and those who would otherwise stand beside them, including the grafted Gentile believers. Israel stands as a prophetic picture of the Body of Christ and a reminder of Satan's imminent defeat; is it any wonder that Satan abhors this race and has many times tried to destroy them?

2. **Abuse of the prophetic gift.** In order to confuse, alienate and destroy, Satan has raised up a counterfeit alongside the prophetic gift the Lord has been restoring to His people. False prophets now control entire people groups and regions that once adhered to God's voice. The antichrist spirit controlling these prophets is leading people further from the truth of the Gospel.

3. **Oppression of women.** Prophetess Cindy Jacobs writes, "Satan cannot afford to have Eden restored and man and woman standing together as they did in the Garden. This would bring order to the home and order to the Church."[5] The enemy's tactic to keep the Church from winning the war and fulfilling the Great Commission

101

is to cause division between the sexes. While we argue over what titles women can and cannot have in ministry, the antichrist spirit renders the Body ineffective for complete victory.

4. **Ethnic domination.** Wherever one ethnic group is dominated by another, the antichrist spirit is in operation. Yet wherever racial reconciliation is occurring, there God is at work. Repentance, which stokes the fires of revival, creates a spirit in direct opposition to that of oppression and domination, which are energized by an antichrist system.

5. **Mammon and iniquitous thrones.** The antichrist system is at work in every society that has allowed sexual immorality to run rampant. The enemy desires to lead people into willful rebellion, wickedness and corruption—all characteristics of perversion. This is not a "private" issue; as perversion becomes the standard in American society, we must understand that this is a demonic structure established to invade every facet of our culture while thwarting God's will.

Since the attacks on the World Trade Center and the Pentagon, which was an attack on the democratic process of America that influences freedom in the world, terrorist attacks and atrocities have become almost a daily affair, from Paris to Libya to Killeen, Texas, to Boston. No place is exempt. These countless attacks did not just happen overnight. Documentaries, commission reports and other research prove these events were well thought out and planned, as Satan was watching for his opportune moment. Yet a spiritual force has been operating behind the scenes for generations. The antichrist system, while present on this earth for thousands of years, is now establishing itself through distinct leaders, nations, economic giants and other influences. Lawlessness does not know boundaries.

The Invasion of the King

And so we are in a battle. You were held captive in the kingdom of darkness, but when you received salvation, God transferred you to the Kingdom of His Son, Jesus. Being in the Kingdom of light brings wonderful blessings. But it also means you have a new enemy. Satan and his forces oppose the Kingdom of light, and that now includes you. That is why God gives you spiritual armor. To prevail against the enemy, you must put on your armor, take up your weapons and stand (see Ephesians 6:10–17). There is a battle raging! Again, choose this day whom you will serve.

Jesus, sent by the Father, came to invade a dark, rebellious world and tear down the works of Satan. Wherever He encountered Satan's works, He tore them down! When He encountered sickness, He released healing. When He encountered lack, He released provision. When He encountered sin, He provided forgiveness and opened a path to righteousness. He came to put an end to Satan's kingdom so the government of heaven could once again be manifested on earth. During the present age, He has called us to join in that work.

Christmas is not just the story of a baby born in Bethlehem. It is not a one-day holiday. Christmas is our need for more of Christ to combat darkness. It is about the invasion of the King over all systems! Heaven invading earth, light invading darkness, warfare and overcoming, redemption and enlistment—the world can be chaotic, but God wants us to remember that the King has come. We are in a battle, but our triumph is assured.

Dr. Robert Heidler, one of the most gifted teachers I know, put it this way to me:

> Some Scripture versions translate John 1:5 as "The light shines in the darkness, and the darkness did not *overcome* it." But other versions say, "The light shines in the darkness, and the darkness did not *comprehend* it." Which is right? They both are! The word means both "comprehend" and "overcome." I believe John chose this word to teach us two very important things.
>
> First, the world cannot *comprehend* the light. It cannot understand why anyone would reject pride, ambition and self-seeking, choosing to walk with God in humble faith and trust. The things of God can seem foolish to the world. But the world also cannot *overcome* the light. That means the kingdom of darkness is ultimately doomed to defeat.

The Kingdom of God is here. Jesus calls us to be representatives of His Kingdom and to spread His light wherever we go. God wants you to know the light shines in the darkness, and the darkness *cannot* overcome it! Because the Body of Christ lacks an understanding of the Kingdom, however—living in a fellowship dimension of Church and mostly following the blueprint of the world—we could miss the force and power necessary to advance in this season of conflict.

War is conflict. Conflicts and seasons of war raise a need for warriors, but as anyone who has fought in battle can attest, simply being a warrior does not guarantee victory against the opponent. Winning takes skilled warriors. In this season, skilled Kingdom warriors must arise to stand in the gaps where evil reigns in the earth. These warriors must contend for peace and wholeness as the forces of darkness close in with increasing strength and skill.

In such a time of direct conflict, how are we to process the wars and rumors of war that surround us? How do we deal with the warfare of one kingdom against another—both spiritual and physical? With the world around us changing rapidly, what will the war look like in the future? How can we become mighty warriors in a Kingdom above all earthly kingdoms, so that we might establish that Kingdom on earth? As we move forward and establish God's presence, we will have to answer these questions, and we will begin to do so in this book.

A Modern Nation of Covenant and War

To understand war, we as God's children must understand the God of Israel, a nation that belongs to Him yet lives in war. We will discuss Israel as God's covenant nation, but for now let me share about two of my children, who have lived in many cities of Israel over several years. Amber Pierce, my son's wife, recounts the following experience with war. As you read her story, I think you will identify with it.

> In the summer of 2014, Israel experienced a fifty-day war. Though God had showed me in the spring that we would enter this time of violence, I was not prepared emotionally for what came.
>
> One day during this war, I had decided that we would have a peaceful evening at home—after putting the kids to bed, we would open a bottle of wine and watch a funny movie. Just after Daniel, my husband, left to walk to the German Colony for a bottle of wine (it is a popular neighborhood in Jerusalem where we used to live), the sirens sounded.

I carried Lily and Elijah down five flights of stairs. Within a minute we began to hear screams from outside and inside our building. I knew this attack was different. I began to pray in my spirit, and then we heard the explosions very nearby. Lily asked me if I thought that her dad was still alive. I wasn't convinced myself, but I did what any good mother would and said, "Yes!"

During attacks in Israel, we are advised to stay in the bomb shelter for ten minutes from the sound of the last explosion. Because of the screaming, I wondered if the building next door had been hit and if there were casualties. In my mind, out of fear, I was convinced that Daniel had been hurt or worse. When these attacks happen, cell phones are often interrupted for a few minutes, and we have to wait to check in with our loved ones.

Finally, a couple of very long minutes later, I received my call from Daniel. He was fine. He asked me to come outside to see the smoke billowing directly over our home. Three rockets the size of telephone poles had been intercepted by the Iron Dome, a missile intercept structure developed partly by the United States. Debris was everywhere!

This attack was too close. I felt I just couldn't commit to this war. This led to a massive argument between Daniel and me. I threw together some diapers, wipes and formula and grabbed Lily and Elijah. We jumped in the first taxi I saw, and, against Daniel's judgment, caught the first plane out of Israel. In my mind I was trying to protect my kids. Daniel saw things differently; he knew we would be fine if we stayed in Jerusalem.

This wasn't our first war. We had previously lived two years in Beersheva (Beersheba) on the southern border of Israel. War was the norm then. It was not unusual to have twenty rockets land close to our home. We felt the vibrations, and everything in the house would shake. At the time I handled these attacks quite well. What I didn't realize until the summer of 2014 was that I had much trauma from that time. Once we moved to Jerusalem, I decided that I was done with war. I made this decision even though God had shown me in a dream that war was coming to Jerusalem as soon as we moved there.

After this close encounter, I fled the war zone and went home with our two children to "safe and sound" Texas, while Daniel stayed in Jerusalem. After spending one week with my mother- and father-in-law, I chose to go back, solely out of my desire to be with Daniel. While in Texas, I had stopped watching the news and convinced myself that Israel was in a cease-fire. As soon as I got on the plane to Tel Aviv with my children, a man informed me that we had just put "boots on the ground" in Israel—we were in full-blown war. But the plane took off and there was no turning back. As I reflected on the plane, I came to the conclusion that war is inescapable.

Returning to Daniel was great. He had gifts for us, and even though we were under a haze of war, being together was all that mattered. Chuck and Pam, along with a team from Glory of Zion, flew to Israel when no one was flying to Israel. They came to worship and prophetically decree the issues of war into the atmosphere of the land. I was still unsettled, but Daniel pressed through to host this first worship meeting in Jerusalem.

The gathering was truly historic! Nothing else was going on in the country at the time, and all of Israel was desperate to join together for prayer and worship. People in Israel often say that you must stay in a place of worship if you are going to live there. Worship and the joy of abiding in the Lord are the only things that sustain you in war! I have learned the joy of worshiping in the midst of war.

This experience has taught me more about the supernatural and the natural becoming the same. In my spirit, I knew something had shifted when the war began, and I felt as if I were coming undone. God had told me that I would have to learn to walk steadily, even on shaky ground, and I knew I had to press on. I believe this is a word for all of us. I have pressed over the past year to find stability. I have realized that to be strengthened for the future we must walk in discipline. I have visualized the hand of God touching the place in my heart that gets wound up. When I feel stirred, I say, "Jesus, touch my heart." I am doing this all through the day, and God is ministering to me and making me strong for the future. I share this because I don't believe that I am the only person going through this process. God is removing things that would keep us from entering into our promises, equipping us for what we will need in the future.

Will a New Generation of Warriors Arise?

The book of Judges encompasses a dark period of the history of Israel. When I look at the world today, I think of many instances in the book of Judges. Much disobedience to the Law of God is recorded, resulting in oppression and death. Joshua's forty-year leadership is almost overpowered by the darkness of the time. The book of Judges also, however, shows God's faithfulness to His covenant when His people repent and turn from their wicked ways. Disastrous consequences follow when we break fellowship with God through idolatrous worship. This is an important principle in understanding warfare.

Romans 6:23 states that the wages of sin is death. That is New Covenant theology. Death is our last enemy. Therefore, when we sin and death abounds, we must go to war. In Judges 3:1–6, we find this synopsis:

Now these are the nations which the LORD left, that He might test Israel by them, that is, all who had not known

108

any of the wars in Canaan (this was only so that the generations of the children of Israel might be taught to know war, at least those who had not formerly known it), namely, five lords of the Philistines, all the Canaanites, the Sidonians, and the Hivites who dwelt in Mount Lebanon, from Mount Baal Hermon to the entrance of Hamath. And they were left, that He might test Israel by them, to know whether they would obey the commandments of the LORD, which He had commanded their fathers by the hand of Moses. Thus the children of Israel dwelt among the Canaanites, the Hittites, the Amorites, the Perizzites, the Hivites, and the Jebusites. And they took their daughters to be their wives, and gave their daughters to their sons; and they served their gods.

The Lord leaves enemies in the land to teach us how to engage in battle and learn how to be victorious. Will we trust Him to overcome and triumph? Will we submit to His strategies? Or will we fall to all the temptations of the enemies who rule in our midst? Just as the Spirit of the Lord came upon Mary, the Spirit of the Lord visited during this dark time: Judges 3:10 says, "The Spirit of the LORD came upon [Othniel], and he judged Israel. He went out to war, and the LORD delivered Cushan-Rishathaim king of Mesopotamia into his hand; and his hand prevailed over Cushan-Rishathaim." Othniel was raised up to bring rest to the land in the midst of all the warfare.

Will a new generation of warriors arise in days ahead? To answer that question, they will have to answer these:

- Will they learn to war in the midst of the enemies that the previous generations left in the land?
- Will they allow the sword of His Word to work deeply within them so the grace of that Word works outwardly?

- Will they be success-driven to accomplish God's King-dom purposes?
- Will they be conformed to the blueprint of the world controlled by mammon?
- Will they learn the increase of God's government or be dependent on civil government?
- Will they have a desire to experience the Lord's glory more than anything in their lives?
- Will they go to war to see His glory established in society?

If we win the war in this generation, the one that follows will experience blessings. The enemy still believes he has a right to shut the portals of heaven so that we, God's children, will be confined to a decaying earth realm where death casts a shadow. Not so! God has made all wisdom available for His children.

We can access that wisdom now. We can ascend into heav-enly places and gain what is necessary to release in the earth. As blood-bought, redeemed children of a Holy God, we can wield the sword of the Spirit in the earth and declare, "On earth as it is in heaven!" Though the enemy has attempted to prevent God's blessings from manifesting, we can prepare a way for those blessings to be revealed.

This is a crucial time for believers. We have the opportunity to be as "wise as serpents" (Matthew 10:16) by being like the sons of Issachar, who served as counselors to King David and had understanding of the times (1 Chronicles 12:32). We also must discern the times, taking full advantage of the otherworldly wisdom God offers us. When we do, we will be prepared for the unfolding wars of our time.

We war as an army as the people of God. Yet we also war as individual soldiers, commissioned by our heavenly Father to possess the land He has given each of us. In these crucial times, you will find it necessary to know how to wage war on *both* fronts. Let violent praise be a standard. Resist the enemy's plans to draw you into passivity, and learn how to enter into any situation and allow the high praises of God to change the atmosphere. He has a battle plan that will pave the way for you to possess your inheritance. So take a deep breath, and let's enter into the unfolding war ahead. You are God's warrior for the future!

Protect Your Vineyard

There is a new call to watch the vineyard you have been given. You must protect your vineyard from the many enemies that would rob you from seeing His blessing occur during this hour. Political structures could rob you of your inheritance at this time.

Recently, before I was to lead a prayer gathering, the Spirit of God spoke to me:

> *Protect your vineyard! Get it cleared, plowed and ready to plant. I am removing one hedge to build another. Ask Me to remove the seeds that will produce wild grapes, rebellious structures and iniquitous thrones in the portion that you have been allotted. Be a watchman over your portion. I am watching over the earth and reviewing My plan of fullness. I am changing the horizon of My people! Their vision must shift to see what I am seeing. I must now address enemies in the land, or the land will be overtaken and its productivity for the next three generations lost. I am going deep to pull up roots that will produce rebellion in days ahead. My people will be revolutionary in a time of lawless rebellion! Declare that the uprooting has begun in your house, your land and the industry you are part of. Thank Me for the uprooting of seeded,*

111

twisted, unfruitful systems and structures that could prevent My Kingdom people from becoming radiant in the future.

I am passing out new assignments. I am causing you to hear what I am assigning you to. Some will be assigned to nations. Others will be assigned to kingdoms, others to companies, others to churches and others to cities. I will assign some to one person, who will open up your future as you pray for him or her. New assignments are coming this hour.

See the fields I am calling you to. Many will be called, placed and planted in new fields. From these new fields you will see the boundaries I have for your future. Many of these fields are undefined. I will show you where to build a hedge.

I have begun to tear down hedges! I am reestablishing the fields of harvest. While tearing down the hedges, I am uprooting the plants that will not produce fruit for the future. This is a time to pluck up and pull out. I am setting you in these opened-up fields to be My farmers for this season. Learn the laws of harvest. Some of you will be plowers and some will be reapers. Many walls were built high in the last season around fields that I had planted, but wild grapes came up. Now I must tear down old fortresses and cause old structures to fall. I will begin to go in now and redo fields. You have been trying to secure the fields from the past season! But now, hedges are falling and the fields that you have been working hard to secure will be replowed and planted with new grain. They will have a new form of harvest. They will be plowed in new ways.

Get ready; in your confusion, the tearing down is part of the process. When I asked you to go forth into the fields the last time, I found you under a shade tree saying, "Why, Lord, are You doing things this way?" I am moving you out from under the shade. Shake off your self-pity and allow My light of revelation to fall on you. Some of you feel exposed. You are not sure where your boundaries are because I am changing them. New fruit is being developed. I can graft, prune and graft again to produce new fruit from old vineyards.

Do not kick against the pricks! The new boundaries and assignments that I am forming around you are key for you to submit to. You had no idea what it would look like when I began to remove and reseed the earth for the harvest ahead. I am beginning to do that. I am giving out new assignments for prayer. You must get your assignment and pray for new industries to form. You must pray during this reorganization of industry. Do not just hang on to your job; come to Me in these days of changing structures. I must transplant and redo many industries, for many iniquities have been held in the industries that produced the movement of the last season. Now I must redo. Some of you are going through a great emotional crisis in your process of being transplanted. Wait! Do not wither in this season. Your roots will go downward and produce fruit upward.

There is deeper oil that I am bringing forth. It has been held for the season ahead. I must go at a different angle to penetrate into and catch that oil and bring it forth. Do not be afraid to invest in the deeper drilling. It will produce a flow that will sustain you in the next season. Like Jonah, who sat under the shade tree, some of you have not liked what I am doing. I have used you to prophesy to set an order and to create a tearing down and uprooting. You have gotten upset in the changes around you. I will dry up what you are hiding under. Rejoice in the changes I am bringing that will produce great fruit in days ahead.

I am calling forth rivers of healing. Many of you have not been able to see the river. Rivers that have nourished crops and brought healing have dried up. My people must find My healing river. I will shake up the fields. I am shaking up your field! The river is hidden. It is very deep. Deep must call to deep. The river must rise again! There must be a river of healing in certain fields before I can move forward. You have turned toward healing. Your healing process is creating a great shaking. This shaking is tearing the walls of the vineyard. Now new vineyards must be established. The river of My power was captured in the last season. A war formed over the movement of the river, and it became a dry bed. I must watch for the times to break the captivity of the healing river. My healing river must flow into new areas to heal the people and the earth.

New instruments are forming. You did not understand the type of instruments I would need in this season. In My reforming, you have not understood what you are going through. I am making new instruments to plow new ground. You must change your vision at this time for your field. Assignments are also changing, as are My instruments. I must plow up ground that had wrong seeds, wild roots and bad fruit. The land is crying out to produce its harvest, but you must allow Me to purify the land. "If My people who are called by My name will humble themselves and pray and turn from their wicked ways and seek My face, then I will hear from heaven and forgive their sin and heal their land."

You have entered an uprooting season, and roots that have been hidden must be found. Your days of communion are changing. Your prayer life will shift. Let Me show you how to pray in different ways, new ways. This was the root that first evangelized the world. Now, that root structure is changing, and you will be affected. Ask Me to cause a wall to be torn down and removed. You are dealing with little foxes, and I want to change the whole field. The little foxes will crush the grapes, and I have got to plow the whole field again. There will be a healing move in those of Scottish descent.

Do not despise small beginnings! I will sow new seeds in those fields. They will come up small, but they will become very fruitful in days ahead. Some of you are not seeing the smallness of the seed that I will plant. A different vine must be released to produce the fruit for this season. This is a season of pruning and grafting and regrafting. Do not focus on the plant. If you are looking at the plant, you could align with Saul, who had "the look." The top of a plant is not the key, since what nourishes it is under the dirt. You must learn to see and eat the root that has gone deep. If you are not careful, you will focus on the Saul system and look at appearance, as opposed to the stream and the root of Judah that must spring forth this hour. I must shift you, for you are operating from eyesight instead of seeing My root blessing. I am moving from one layer, and I am going deeper.

You have been speaking from the surface of your emotions, but I am going deep into the very depths of your heart so you speak forth. Even the songs and the prophecies and that which I have given you have been at one level, but now I am going down into a place that you have never had unlocked. It will nurture what I want to produce this hour. I am unlocking the next song for you to sing. I am going deeper to unlock a valve and connect with a river that will produce a different type of song.

The furnace of My fire is much greater than hell's lickings. I am causing you to go into the kiln of My process at this time to fire you and make you glazed and radiant so that I can use you as a vessel in days ahead. I will fire nations this year. I will cause things to happen that will create a furnace in nations. In the midst of that, I will bring forth those who are tested and tried. Do not balk when I assign you to be at the ticket counter. Yes, you have great abilities, but there is a reason I have placed you there. Quit despising your position so that I can rebuild the hedge of the place where I will plant you in days ahead.

Bless Me at every small beginning. You will see a river producing nutrients at one level, but a fire is down deep that will bring about germination. Where hell has licked your feet and your process from the last season, you will see the fire of hell and will know how to distinguish it in the flow of the fruit that I will bring forth in the next season. I will bring forth songs that will quench hell's fires in the next season. My people are not aware of the changing structures, and they are grieving and in denial because the structures are changing. I am going to go deeper to produce the songs to show them the depth that I can bring forth on their behalf.

The fruit of the blessing is in the root. This is why I prune the fruit and branches. What needs to be lopped off in appearance will be lopped off. You have looked at the appearance, but I am going deeper so that the blessing is connected rightly and will come forth in a new way. The blessing is the fruit that grows from the root. When your root goes deep and draws from the river of My anointing and presence, My blessing cannot help but come.

I will pluck up certain things this year and leave other things in the ground. I am digging and redoing the field. I am resetting the hedge. Do not move quickly in the plucking up. Many of the root systems that I have are entwined with evil systems that must gently be removed. Turn your face to the fire. You have tried to run and leave the fire. Turn your face to the fire and watch the burning and clearing, for the wind of My Spirit is in the fire this hour. I must send forth the burning so there will not be an evil root left. For those who fear My name, I will rise over you as the sun of righteousness. That is where your shade will come forth. I will rise again, so turn your face to the fire. Face the wind of the fire, and in the midst of the cleansing, I will rise again.

Turn your face to the fire and receive your health. Turn your face to the fire and receive your cure. Turn your face to the fire and deliverance will come. My refreshing is in this fire. The sun of righteousness will rise over you, and you will stand in the land with a new stand. The healing in My wings will restore your fields. Turn your face to the fire in your field and watch Me burn away that which would keep you from moving under My wing of healing. Do not resist the burning of the field. Turn your face to the fire, for that is where you will be healed. Many snakes have been in your field, and by the cleansing of the field the snakes will be seen and will leave your field. Turn your face to the fire, and My peace will rise up in you. I am in a repair mode, and I must burn away and remove so I can repair. Turn your face to the fire, and I will repair your broken wing.

Keep turning until you have turned into the new path ahead. Do not let the enemy wear you down. The Lord is taking us back to the blessing of the root. That is why some of you are not seeing the blessing you need to see—you need to go back to the blessing of the root!

War from the root of the issue that you know should be overturned. Do not just look at the top or appearance of a thing, but look at the root. Ask Him to restore any root system that has been overtaken by darkness. Ask Him to dig around, fertilize and water the seeds that are deep within you. Ask for Him to strengthen what remains. Do not grow weary! You will triumph in the midst of changing trends. Pray in such a way that you receive revelation for the battle, and live in such a way that you withstand the schemes of the enemy!

5

Authority to Overthrow Iniquitous Thrones

Did you know that you have a portion specifically allotted to you from God? The word *inheritance* means "my portion." We have all been given a space, territory or arena in which we have been granted authority. That is our portion, and how we steward it is key to our success in the spirit realm. In fact, the climate of our domain reflects our relationship with the Lord; therefore, our chief desire should be for the presence of the Holy God to occupy our inheritance. You must learn to war to see His presence in your entire sphere of authority.

In 2000, as I was writing the first book in this series, I prophesied about the coming war season. I focused on the United States because we Americans always seemed to think that harm was beyond our borders, yet I knew that physical attacks were ahead for us. I shared publicly that I felt the first attack would be in New York City because of its large Jewish population. (At that time, New York City had the second-highest population of Jews in the world, after Tel Aviv.)

When three commercial airplanes with suicide pilots approached the World Trade Center and the Pentagon (with a fourth destroyed in a fiery crash in a Pennsylvania field), the world as we knew it changed. The resulting disintegration of the Twin Towers and loss of approximately 3,000 lives propelled the United States—and the rest of the world—into an unprecedented season of conflict that has escalated over the past several years.

The spiritual could be discerned from the physical: The attack in New York became a physical manifestation of the new season we entered into. A new type of war had begun, with everyday tools used for weapons. Some were even willing to lay down their lives for what they believed. The war of faith had begun!

The Church in America began to wake up to warfare and the choice to war or not to war. Previously, the Church had been lulled into apathy; actually, many had become antiwar out of fear and in need of accommodating religion. I hope the last chapter nullified this misconception, as it is essential for Christians to understand warfare and take up their weapons. The Lord is raising up a new type of Kingdom warrior who will overcome and triumph. We will become a triumphant band that accesses heaven and unlocks the resources of earth.

Awakening to the Spiritual Unseen War

The Lord had begun to do this very work in me years earlier. Warfare understanding became a must, for I had watched our family unit disintegrate in the 1960s. It was a season of great conflict and change in the world, and our family seemed to personify the season. My dad died an untimely, violent death in 1970. The hopes of prosperity for three generations hung in the balance.

In 1972, the Spirit of God visited me for the first time. I had met Him, but did not know the power of His presence, and I had not really been engulfed by His Spirit. When this happened, my awareness of His presence became a conviction. I began to commune with Him in a new way. I could see His glory moving. To this day, I have not regressed to where I was before this visitation. I share this because the family is the first war unit, and we must learn to war for the immediate spheres in which God has placed us.

I began to learn and recognize His voice. As I delved into the Word of God, the Bible ceased to be a mere story; rather the life of the Word was imputed to me. I could sense His Spirit in me. I asked Him questions and heard Him speak. I knew I was to obey what I heard.

I remember asking Him what had happened in my family, and He flashed a scene in my mind. I saw the heart of my family, and then He revealed the bloodline of the heart of the family flowing into my own heart. I could see that I was allowing glory to push darkness out of my heart. Each time my heart beat, His Spirit flowing through my blood pushed out and eradicated the darkness that was hidden.

The Lord then opened my eyes to something that would change me forever. He showed me *Satan's toe* stuck in a portion of my heart, and I understood two things: I saw the reality of Satan's being and how he infiltrates those who give him permission; he was actually occupying a portion of me. I also knew I had to go to war to remove his toehold from the heart of our family.

Beginning to war brought supernatural manifestations.[1] Warfare became a reality, as my personal war led me to understand corporate, territorial and generational warfare. The Lord revealed a key as I learned discernment for the future: *The absence of the presence of God indicates the working of a curse.*

My whole life has been about overturning iniquitous structures in my bloodline that captured great potential in other generations. I began to see the working of demonic hosts, how they were set against God's plan for my family, and the destiny that God had ordained before the foundation of the world. The Lord showed me that if I would war for the overthrow of these iniquities in my bloodline, He would use me for the "healing of the nations." The story of the minas in Luke 19 became a reality: If we are stewards with the small and the first, God will multiply us by entrusting to us cities and nations.

A Core That Cannot Be Shaken

I cried out to the Lord for help. He answered, *Greater am I in you. Allow the greater to overtake the lesser! Raise up a standard and develop a core that is unshakable.* He then said, *I can restore all that you have lost!*

A *core* is a central and foundational part of the whole. It is distinct from the developing part, shapes the interior and conducts necessary strength and structure to the whole. The core is the innermost enduring part from which the movement and stability of all other parts develop. I knew the Lord was saying that His Word was to become my backbone, so that I could withstand everything attempting to overthrow my destiny. I also knew that His strength would enable me to restore all that should have been. I knew that I never had to submit to evil; I was meant to overthrow evil.

As I studied the Word of God, core Scriptures were added to the mindset that the Spirit of God was forming in me. He had already revealed Proverbs 3 to me supernaturally. I was the firstborn son in my family, and He had shown me the concept of firstfruits. He then instructed me from this passage not to lean on my own understanding and to flee from evil. He was revealing to me what evil was really like. I then began a journey to develop the core inside me that would be unshakable against the onslaughts of the enemy. My first step was to set up a standard of the Word of God in me around which all things in life would revolve.

As He began to add His Word of life in me, the Word became my first weapon of defense against the enemy. Fourteen key Scriptures became like the very core of my being. The number fourteen in the Word of God is linked with deliverance and developing a testimony in the midst of your boundaries of operation.

I suggest you do the same thing. Stop and list the core development Scriptures within you that cause you to overcome. My own were as follows:

> Trust in the LORD with all your heart, and lean not on your own understanding; in all your ways acknowledge Him, and He shall direct your paths. Do not be wise in your own eyes; fear the LORD and depart from evil. It will be health to your flesh, and strength to your bones. Honor the LORD with your possessions, and with the firstfruits of all your increase; so your barns will be filled with plenty, and your vats will overflow with new wine.
>
> Proverbs 3:5–10

I will bless those who bless you, and I will curse him who curses you; and in you all the families of the earth shall be blessed.

Genesis 12:3

The spirit of a man will sustain him in sickness, but who can bear a broken spirit?

Proverbs 18:14

This Book of the Law shall not depart from your mouth, but you shall meditate in it day and night, that you may observe to do according to all that is written in it. For then you will make your way prosperous, and then you will have good success.

Joshua 1:8

And it shall come to pass afterward that I will pour out My Spirit on all flesh; your sons and your daughters shall prophesy, your old men shall dream dreams, your young men shall see visions.

Joel 2:28

For the word of God is living and powerful, and sharper than any two-edged sword, piercing even to the division of soul and spirit, and of joints and marrow, and is a discerner of the thoughts and intents of the heart.

Hebrews 4:12

So then faith comes by hearing, and hearing by the word of God.

Romans 10:17

For in Christ Jesus neither circumcision nor uncircumcision avails anything, but faith working through love.

Galatians 5:6

How much more shall the blood of Christ, who through the eternal Spirit offered Himself without spot to God, cleanse your conscience from dead works to serve the living God? And for this reason He is the Mediator of the new covenant, by means of death, for the redemption of the transgressions under the first covenant, that those who are called may receive the promise of the eternal inheritance.

Hebrews 9:14–15

For sin shall not have dominion over you, for you are not under law but under grace.

Romans 6:14

He who sins is of the devil, for the devil has sinned from the beginning. For this purpose the Son of God was manifested, that He might destroy the works of the devil.

1 John 3:8

Now you are the body of Christ, and members individually. And God has appointed these in the church: first apostles, second prophets, third teachers, after that miracles, then gifts of healings, helps, administrations, varieties of tongues.

1 Corinthians 12:27–28

The heavens declare the glory of God; and the firmament shows His handiwork. Day unto day utters speech, and night unto night reveals knowledge. There is no speech nor language where their voice is not heard. Their line has gone out through all the earth, and their words to the end of the world. In them He has set a tabernacle for the sun, which is like a bridegroom coming out of his chamber, and rejoices like a strong man to run its race. Its rising is from one end of heaven, and its circuit to the other end; and there is nothing hidden from its heat. The law of the LORD is perfect, converting the soul; the testimony of the LORD is sure, making wise the simple.

Psalm 19:1–7

And blessed is he who is not offended because of Me.

Matthew 11:6

I write out these words using whatever Bible version I am reading through that year. I also use the Scriptures to write a prophecy that applies to me for the year to come. Since this prophecy is based on the Hebraic calendar, each year the prophecy is different. The Word is multifaceted, and without a vision (prophetic utterance), the people perish, or go backward (see Proverbs 29:18). From the time that the Lord overwhelmed me at eighteen years of age, I purposed never to go backward!

After I had spent three years reading the Bible and learning to meditate on His Word, something happened. Scriptures that did not mention war became weapons in my hand to combat the spiritual forces linked with my bloodline. The Lord began to lead me in an incredible way and has continued daily to guide me into His path of righteousness. He has taught me to embrace His Spirit; to be quick to hear and slow to speak; how to discern using both Word and Spirit; the necessity of worship in Spirit and truth; the five-fold gifts of God's Kingdom rule; the power of the restoration of the Tabernacle of David and how sound creates movement; and Antichrist's antics against Kingdom harvest. I will explain more as you continue reading.

Decreeing, Declaring and Proclaiming

God has chosen His people to be the bridge that brings His will from heaven to earth. He wants us to commune with

Him, listen carefully to His voice, gain prophetic revelation and decree that revelation into the earth. The atmosphere of earth responds when we speak what heaven is saying. This unlocks miracles and releases His blessings.

Once we hear God, not only can we intercede, but we can prophesy. As I wrote in chapter 1, prophesying is declaring His mind and His heart. We are His voice in His earth. As we speak, He forms His will in the earth. We should always be willing to say yes and amen to His promises. When we receive prophetic revelation, we need to decree it. I often speak out the following verses, especially when I minister from place to place:

> I will declare the decree: The LORD has said to Me . . .
>
> Psalm 2:7

> You will make your prayer to Him, and He will hear you, and you will pay your vows. You shall also decide and decree a thing, and it shall be established for you; and the light [of God's favor] shall shine upon your ways. When they make [you] low, you will say, [There is] a lifting up; and the humble person He lifts up and saves. He will even deliver the one [for whom you intercede] who is not innocent; yes, he will be delivered through the cleanness of your hands.
>
> Job 22:27–30 AMPC

> Then He saw wisdom and declared it; He prepared it, indeed, He searched it out.
>
> Job 28:27

A decree is an official order, edict or decision that appears to be foreordained; this is what makes decrees prophetic. The word *decree* can also mean to order, decide or officially appoint a group or person to accomplish something—to set apart or ordain something or someone.

A declaration is an announcement, a formal statement or a proclamation; such a statement is released by a plaintiff in his complaint to bring about a court action. A proclamation actually brings something into a more official realm. A proclamation can ban, outlaw or restrict, which is linked to binding and loosing.

All through the Word of God you find decrees, declarations and proclamations: Cyrus sent out a decree that brought God's people back from captivity to rebuild Jerusalem and the Temple of God. Caesar decreed a census that positioned Mary and Joseph in the place where prophecy could be fulfilled through the birth of Jesus. Elijah declared that the heavens would be shut up. The priests proclaimed what God was ordaining. Once we hear the word of the Lord decreed, declared or proclaimed, God begins to establish this word in the earth realm. This causes God's people to press in for a full manifestation of what He is longing to accomplish in our midst.

We are in a time of prophetic declaration and apostolic proclamation. God's people are becoming bold to say what He is saying. As I explain in chapter 1, this creates an open heaven and brings heaven and earth into agreement. I call this an open portal or door in heaven. When you proclaim the following prophetic decree over your region and the Body of Christ, action will be taken in your atmosphere:

> *My river is changing course. Ready yourself for the next war! Do not remain in your last war cycle. Make sure you are allowing or causing or choosing for the old to end. Deal with all of your dangerous emotions so they will not present great challenges to you in the future. Move into your next phase of victory!*

128

Receive a new anointing. This is a season of victory over death cycles and the fear of death. This will produce victory over demonic forces that would try to stop you in the future. This is not a season of decrease but increase and harvest. Decree and prepare your storehouse to be filled. Receive a supernatural anointing to interpret the times. Move in My timing and prosper.

When the enemy encircles you, declare you will find security in the Lord. The enemy will attempt to surround you, so be sure to develop your shields of protection. Musk oxen form a circle around a cow that is giving birth. This provides protection so the next generation can come forth. My watchman and intercessory army must be like the musk ox in their regions.

Be surrounded and sealed by the Holy Spirit. Develop a new level of discernment through worship. Reality is produced when you worship in Word (truth) and Spirit. Do not cycle through your wilderness again. Break the cycle of Mount Sinai. (Do not go around that mountain again!) Head upward to Mount Zion. In the face of your enemy, praise violently! Let praise bind the strongman and then plunder, take and repossess your spoils. Come full circle. I will give you a second chance to confront and deal with that thing that defeated you in the last season. Submit and take this opportunity. This will stop you from going around that same mountain again.

Let Me take My compass and drop My plumb line in your midst. Allow Me to set a new direction and chart your course for the future (see 1 Corinthians 16:5–18). *Do not fear; go up against what has seemed invincible in your past* (see Joshua 5–7). *Let My supernatural love overwhelm and encompass you. This will release a dimension of compassion and faith that the Church has lost and cause the healing mantle to be restored to her; this will open the door for prodigals to return* (see Matthew 9; Luke 15).

Review your boundaries. This is a season of divine commandments. I will restructure your boundaries so the Law can be fulfilled in your hearts. This will allow you to take back the ground from the enemy who has shifted laws and time (see Daniel 7:25). *Ask Me to bring forth new revelation from the pulpit of your region. Supernatural teaching will defy religion. I will reveal a different dimension of the Word to expound upon* (see Mark 2). *This is a season of My Spirit supernaturally rekindling the power gifts. The war will take a supernatural turn* (see 1 Corinthians 12, 14). *(Example: There is a fine line between words of knowledge and ESP. Both operate the same way, but their inspiration comes from different sources—words of knowledge from Holy Spirit, ESP by accessing familiar and familial spirits to bring forth knowledge.)*

Worship Me with a new expression of worship. Be expressive in praise and rejoice in the midst of your battles. Do not hide your emotions (see 2 Chronicles 20). *The roar of the Lion of Judah will win your battles! Declare the generations will connect and war together* (see Isaiah 59:15–21). *Generations will circle together and bring forth a new victory. Recover your losses and plunder. Take authority over your emotions* (read Exodus 3–12; 1 Samuel 30). *Gain new prayer strategies, prepare the way and expect victory. Do not let the enemy's retaliation cause you to back up.*

Know that warfare is intensifying throughout the earth. In the midst of warfare, come up! Ascend under the shadow of My wing and war from the abiding place that I have prepared for you! Stand still, cease and desist from striving and worship Me!

Many blessings in heavenly places are accessible to God's men and women of faith. To access these blessings, however, we must at times topple the throne that attempts to block God's Kingdom government. With war and rumors of war flying around the world, it is important that, as God's people, we remind ourselves that we can have peace in the midst of war. The war is a supernatural, spiritual war, not just a war against flesh and blood. We must also remind ourselves that the war is a worship war. Who will be worshiped? We declare that our God is worthy to be worshiped!

The War of Thrones

The only entity on earth that has power to break strongholds of the enemy's domain is the Church. The only person with this power is the Holy Spirit. When we allow Him to move in the Church, the Church is empowered.

Satan's objective is to block the plan of God by establishing his legal right to control an area. Satan gains access into an area the same way he gains access into an individual's life or family: through sin. He seeks to escalate individual or family sin into corporate sin. When corporate sin enters into our assigned boundaries, it can build a throne of iniquity, and we need to be aware of how we, positioned in God's army, have the authority to dismantle it.

Our sin affects even the ground within our sphere of authority. Sin creates a break in God's purpose and order. When these breaks occur, Satan takes advantage and begins to establish his influence in an area. From that place of influence, Satan can actually build a throne on which he is seated in a territory. We see this in Revelation 2:13: "I know your works, and where you dwell, where Satan's throne is."

In exalting himself, Satan is attempting to draw all people to his counterfeit light. He knows that all people are created to be vessels of worship and that, whether or not they realize it, they will worship something. They will either worship the true and living God or they will worship Satan and his demonic forces, whether overtly or through sin (whether sin of omission or commission). It is this "worship" of corporate sin that builds the throne on which Satan is seated; from that throne demonic forces work to perpetuate the sin and establish the throne of iniquity to an even greater extent.

Now is the time to understand and overthrow the thrones of iniquity that are ruling and influencing the earth. God is calling His Church into a new and intimate place where the anointing will break the yoke and overturn the structures holding many captive. God is stirring up His people's faith and releasing a gift of faith to break the power of generational iniquitous patterns that have stopped families from experiencing the blessings of God. He is empowering people with faith to see His glory spread throughout cities, regions and states.

The Church must now war to come out of its status quo and into a new structure that presents the Gospel to a lost and dying world. Just as the structure was new in the first century, it is being reformed to meet the needs of the world in the twenty-first century. We must change into a vibrant, fire-filled army marching forward. This call to advance will transform the Body of Christ into a vibrant worshiping force. This is a time to enthrone Christ as king so that other thrones will topple.

Fill the Gaps

The Lord seeks those who will stand in gaps until the breaches are filled and the wall is rebuilt—and we are those people. A gap is the place of disconnect between heaven and earth. Injustices occur in the gaps, and the demonic operates. When we cannot stand, the Lord tells us to stand anyway (see Ephesians 6).

It is time to go up into the gaps (see Ezekiel 13:5) and block Satan's opportunity. In Luke 11, we find the model for our prayers, a cry for the Kingdom of God. The Lord's prayer begins, "Our Father Who is in heaven, hallowed be Your name, Your kingdom come. Your will be done [held holy and revered] on earth as it is in heaven" (verse 2 AMPC). We must invite the Spirit of God to build His Kingdom in our hearts, families, churches, cities, states and nations. He longs for His Kingdom rule to reside in the earth realm. It is already here, but not in its fullness—at once *already* and *not yet*. It is here today, yet still to come.

In order to see God's Kingdom come in its fullness, we must understand how to pray and position ourselves for the future. Get ready for a great shaking! Thrones of iniquity are going to fall. We are about to see a tremendous shift in worship throughout the world as God's throne is reestablished and the Church rises into a new glory. We war as an army, as the people of God. Yet we also war as individual soldiers, commissioned by our heavenly Father to possess the land He has given each of us. In these crucial times, you will find it necessary to know how to wage war on *both* fronts. Let violent praise be a standard. Resist the enemy's plans to draw you into passivity. Learn how to enter into any situation and allow the high praises of God to change the atmosphere. He has a battle plan that will pave the way for you to possess your inheritance.

Tearing Down Iniquitous Thrones

There are many aspects and levels of God's administration, but the key to its operation is the five-fold ministry, also known as ascension gifts or foundational gifts. When the Lord Jesus ascended into heaven to be enthroned at the Father's right hand, He released five gifts to us; the purpose of these "ascension" gifts is to establish His Kingdom and equip His Church.

Ephesians 4:11 identifies these five unique ministries as apostle, prophet, teacher, pastor and evangelist. When these gifts are properly aligned and functioning as God intended, we will see David's Tabernacle restored. This is who we are! We are being restored, and we are moving into a new administration in the house, bringing a new Kingdom demonstration. To establish our future, we must understand God's order. We must capture the revelation of God and receive His assignments, such as warring against a spiritual force or praying over a particular place. Without this Kingdom government in place, other governments do not shake; consequently, the victory for which Christ paid the price is not maintained in the earth, and strongholds develop.

I wrote more about strongholds in my book *Time to Defeat the Devil*:

> I define a stronghold as "a thought process implanted by a spiritual force that keeps a person in bondage." . . . Second Corinthians 10:5 tells us that spiritual strongholds are formed by thoughts that raise themselves above and against the knowledge of Christ . . . which means a living and interactive experience of God. . . . Many times the devil will attack this knowledge by exploiting distress, trauma or need. He comes to your mind and begins accusing God before you. He then offers you a solution or way of escape that leaves God out of the process. This eventually leads to greater bondage, as Satan presents you with a way of escape that does not involve intervention by a loving God. . . . On the foundation of this lie, a system of worship is built, for we worship what we serve.[2]

Sadly, rather than recognizing the way of escape that God provides (see 1 Corinthians 10:13), we accept the counterfeit escape from our distress provided by the devil. In fact, many times we will war to keep the devil's escape plan in place, and, in doing so, begin serving the system that holds us in bondage.

When left to develop, a stronghold is used to build a throne of iniquity. This stronghold multiplies and is imparted into the minds of entire groups—this is what happens with any ideology or philosophy. The stronghold is empowered by demons while the groups worship the thoughts behind the structure.

Are We Under Israel's Bondage in Egypt?

Such a stronghold was established in Egypt, when the Israelites were enslaved under an elaborate system of pagan worship for protection from every type of trouble. To break His people out of this stronghold of false worship, God had to demonstrate His power over the gods of Egypt; through the plagues He demolished the pagan stronghold and showed Himself as the God who could protect and deliver them.

This worship of demonic powers in the heavens led to the establishment of thrones of iniquity through the unholy agreement between heaven and earth. God is not interested in sharing His rule with such thrones; as Scripture says in Psalm 94:20, "Shall the throne of iniquity, which devises evil by law, have fellowship with You?" God wants to break the power of demonic thrones by opening up a new way of worship to us. That is why He told Pharaoh to let His people go into the desert so that they might *worship Him there.*

> Whoever is enthroned has the right and power to rule. This was the problem in Egypt before the Exodus. For Israel coming out of Egypt, it was necessary not just to break the power of the gods of Egypt but also to establish a new order of

worship to the Lord. This was God's intent from the beginning. . . . The nation could not be established in the Promised Land until the Lord was enthroned over them.[3]

Elsewhere in Scripture we see thrones of iniquity torn down and true worship of God established in their place. Gideon tore down his own father's altar, freeing the people from its demonic influence and leading to freedom from Midianite oppression as well (see Judges 6). King Hezekiah tore down altars to idols in the land and restored worship of the Lord in the Temple (see 2 Kings 18). Because the Lord's throne had been established during Hezekiah's reign, the Assyrians were not able to defeat Judah.

In every territory, thrones compete against the glory of God infiltrating earth and unlocking the harvest of a generation. Many people, however, do not understand how to pray and war in this area. This is why God is raising up a new army in the earth realm for this age. These triumphant ones will be discussed in the next chapter.

The Lord is extending a fresh call to His people for cities and regions:

> Overcome every obstacle that is keeping people from coming to know Me. Open the door for My House to be built within them so they may experience My love throughout eternity. Through prayer, gain wisdom that will dethrone the thrones of iniquity where they have been established. Then establish My throne that many may worship Me and gain life everlasting!

This is how entire cities will experience conversion. This is also how we will overthrow thrones of iniquity and see God's covenant plan for whole territories flourish in days ahead.

Change the Atmosphere and Occupy the Land

The praise and worship of God's people will literally create a different atmosphere around us, because the Lord comes down and inhabits our worship (see Psalm 22:3). We are entering into the same type of worship season that we have seen in reformatory times. He, the God of the universe, dwells in the midst of our praising Him. It is not hard to imagine, then, why this changes our measure of faith and gives us strength to grab hold of the inheritance He has for us. As a triumphant people, we will overthrow thrones.

> See, I have set the land before you; go in and possess the land which the LORD swore to your fathers—to Abraham, Isaac, and Jacob—to give to them and their descendants after them. . . . Every commandment which I command you today you must be careful to observe, that you may live and multiply, and go in and possess the land of which the LORD swore to your fathers.
>
> Deuteronomy 1:8; 8:1

When we occupy something, we take possession of it or keep it in our possession. In Luke 21:19 Jesus calls us to posses our souls. In warring against the enemies of this age, we must learn how to occupy and possess. This is a season of tearing down three-fold cords. Nations are being realigned, and new allies are aligning for this new season. When we possess the portion that God has for us, we become whole, fulfilled and full of peace. This is what we are actually warring to accomplish! We must settle for nothing less than the abundance the Lord has for us.

6

A Triumphant Army Arising

When people try to communicate the war ahead to those who are not aware, sometimes they find much resistance. I have already discussed the difficulty for Christians in understanding the relationship between spiritual war and physical war. I hope, as you are reading this book, it has helped you better discern the times and understand God's unfolding plan for the coming days. I also believe you are coming to recognize the greatest emerging worldly force of the end times: the antichrist system.

Many times we can see a natural manifestation of what goes on in a spiritual war. When the Body of Christ at large engages in spiritual warfare, all of natural society is affected: religion, politics (legal and military), economics, media, arts and entertainment, family, education. These seven "mountains" or "mind molders" define what society looks like. How we live is linked with the condition of these societal structures. How the Kingdom of God influences these structures determines the righteousness of a society in the earth. For us to influence and make way for His Kingdom to manifest, God raises up *worshiping intercessors* in each of these arenas of power. I believe society is shifting because more people are now interceding. God is raising an army of intercessors who are contending in the heavenly realm and bringing changes to earth. More help must be enlisted, however.

Our Testimony Will Triumph

From season to season, we must be prepared to enter every conflict with a mind for victory. In this season, the Lord is toughening us up. Isaiah 41:10 (AMPC) says,

> Fear not [there is nothing to fear], for I am with you; do not look around you in terror and be dismayed, for I am your God. I will strengthen and harden you to difficulties, yes, I will help you; yes, I will hold you up and retain you with My [victorious] right hand of rightness and justice.

Sometimes we do not understand that the tough circumstances we are confronted with are simply the training tools of God. These circumstances produce a reality of His presence in our lives. They increase spiritual strength within us as we fight against the destructive plans of the enemy to weaken us in the midst of trials.

The key to walking through conflicts is watching for signs that are in your path. Those signs assist you in making the correct decisions that keep moving you toward victory and triumph.

Always remember that testing produces a testimony, and testimony overcomes. Revelation 12:7–12 says,

And war broke out in heaven: Michael and his angels fought with the dragon; and the dragon and his angels fought, but they did not prevail, nor was a place found for them in heaven any longer. So the great dragon was cast out, that serpent of old, called the Devil and Satan, who deceives the whole world; he was cast to the earth, and his angels were cast out with him. Then I heard a loud voice saying in heaven, "Now salvation, and strength, and the kingdom of our God, and the power of His Christ have come, for the accuser of our brethren, who accused them before our God day and night, has been cast down. And they overcame him by the blood of the Lamb and by the word of their testimony, and they did not love their lives to the death. Therefore rejoice, O heavens, and you who dwell in them! Woe to the inhabitants of the earth and the sea! For the devil has come down to you, having great wrath, because he knows that he has a short time."

During trying circumstances, God longs for us to draw strength from His greatness. He wants to be our shield of defense now and forevermore. Indeed, what have we to fear when it is God who commissions us to fight?

Shifting to a Wineskin of Triumph

Every move of God has a timed life. When movement begins to cease, we must wait for a new breath of life to bring new interactions with heaven and manifestations of the Kingdom on earth. One of the most difficult times to shift a mindset is when we have experienced something glorious and the glory begins to ebb. We relish what was and how the power of the glory affected us, but at the same time we must long to experience God in a new way.

141

A great example of this is when God manifested Himself as a cloud and a fire for forty years in the wilderness. Yet when the time came for the Israelites to cross the Jordan into the long-awaited territory of promise, He removed cloud and fire. He then said,

> This is how you will know that the living God [Hebrew: El Chay] is among you…Watch the ark of the promise of the Lord [Hebrew: Adonay] of the whole earth as it goes ahead of you into the Jordan River….The water flowing from upstream will stop and stand up like a dam.
>
> Joshua 3:10–11, 13 GW

In other words, the people had to learn a new manifestation of God. Now they would have to align with the movement of the priests and the Ark—not the cloud and the fire.

The apostolic government of the Church is now maturing. The prayer movement that ushered it in must remain fluid, becoming a drink offering in whatever region we are seeking to welcome His glory. New people in every nation will invest themselves in this emerging movement. Many of you who have been faithful in the past season will find your place in what I call the "wineskin of triumph."

A Nation Birthed in a Day

A prayer movement is the wine for the now-forming wineskin. Though we have had many prayer movements throughout history, none impacted the world like the one orchestrated by Peter and Doris Wagner beginning in the early 1990s and lasting through 2010. This movement encompassed the prayer emphasis for the areas of the world known as the 10/40 Window and 40/70 Window. Teams were mobilized to each nation within these latitudinal and longitudinal boundaries, and fruit from these movements is still being reported.

During that time, Dutch Sheets and I visited all fifty of the United States and Washington, D.C. From state to state in our nation, we gathered, mobilized and synergized prayer warriors and intercessors. These gatherings were to become apostolic, prophetic prototypes in the earth.[1]

When we first began mobilizing intercessors, we knew that each gathering would be a key, identifying those who were passionately seeking the Lord and bringing forth revelation in their region. For our nation, the United States of America, we knew to pray for the Lord to restore the breastplate of righteousness that had been tarnished through corruption and iniquity. Our major goal in these meetings was to realign the Body properly and to decree the Lord's redemptive plan for each state. This would stir up faith in the Body of Christ in each state and awaken believers to take their stand on behalf of their land.

Any nation can be transformed! Isaiah 66:7–11 (GW) tells us,

> Before a woman goes into labor, she gives birth. Before she has labor pains, she delivers a child. Who has heard of such a thing? Who has seen such things? Can a country be born in one day? Can a nation be born in a moment? When Zion went into labor, she also gave birth to her children. "Do I bring a mother to the moment of birth and not let her deliver?" asks the Lord. "Do I cause a mother to deliver and then make her unable to have children?" asks your God. All who love Jerusalem, be happy and rejoice with her. All who mourn for her, be glad with her. You will nurse and be satisfied from her comforting breasts. You will nurse to your heart's delight at her full breasts.

First and foremost, God's order must be established for a nation to be birthed in a day and eventually transformed. When strategic intercessors are aligned with apostolic leaders, breakthrough begins. Intercessors carry the burden of God and bring it through a birthing process. Prophetic people then make key declarations. Apostles set these decrees in motion. Pastors and teachers nurse and mature those that are mobilized. Evangelists, healers and miracle workers are constantly mobilizing more.

Another way of understanding this is that intercessors keep the heavens open, while prophets express God's heart over a nation, city or structure. The prophets make key declarations into the atmosphere. Apostolic leaders use that revelation or blueprint of heaven and bring it into an established form in the earth realm. Then the Body begins to rally and mobilize as the prototype takes shape and accelerates in development.

I have asked many this question: Are you wine or a wineskin? Do you flow predominately in the category called wine (revelation), or are you developing a wineskin for others to pour into? What are you being poured into, or who is pouring into you? You must know your identity. Some people have incredible revelatory gifts; others are involved with developing structures for that revelation to be poured into. A prophet will receive more revelation than an apostolic builder.

God is calling a Kingdom army full of prayer warriors who know their spheres of authority. We are being sent again into society to break Satan's blueprint and transform the way we think! We must embrace the shifting paradigms communicated this hour from heaven. We must assist in the development of strategies to unlock the nations of the earth.

God will use His peculiar people to change the way His Kingdom advances. Are we still praying? The answer is a loud yes! The army of God is daily growing stronger. Ask the Lord to renew your prayer life. Pray with words and pray the Word! Travail also in the Spirit with words unknown. Commune with your Maker and be bold in the earth realm, where you have been positioned as a witness to His love, grace and power. Speak and decree the Word. War with your prophecies! Do not let the confusion around you create a veil of darkness that stops you from moving forward. Yes, we are praying! But now we are not only praying; we are *beginning to move mountains.*

Prayer to Prophecy to Apostolic Execution

At the beginning of the 1990s, the Lord sovereignly positioned me with Mike and Cindy Jacobs. I was a prayer warrior and Cindy an intercessor. She has had great influence in my life. I listen closely when she prophesies, and I heeded this word she released at a leadership gathering:

> It is time to shift the prayer movement. We must become apostolic in our expression. We must find the intercessors and prophets and align them with the apostles in each state. If each leader of the present movement will shift, their state will shift. If this shift does not occur, the Lord's Kingdom will not be established from state to state, and a nation will suffer greatly.[2]

A Kingdom move is occurring in the Church. In the 1990s and even through the year 2010, the Church was still praying in the prayer room. This is a great blessing, but what happens behind the closed doors of our prayer closets, whether individual or corporate, must eventually be shouted from the rooftops. Now is the time to head to the rooftops!

An apostolic governmental anointing in the prayer movement has emerged. Once we gain strategic revelation, what God reveals must be mobilized publicly. As we draw closer to the end times and see spiritual warfare intensify, we need to pray in such a way that we receive revelation for the battle and live in such a way that we withstand the schemes of the enemy.

A Vision of a New Movement

In September 2007, the Lord alerted me to a change in my life and its direction. He said, *Lay down your involvement in the prayer movement. I am going to reposition you and show you what is to come in days ahead. The prayer movement needs to be the wine for the wineskin that is forming. Look ahead to see a new wineskin.*

I did not know where the Lord intended to reposition me, so through the fall and winter and into spring, I continued to minister as the Lord led me. Then, on May 31, 2008, I joined John and Sheryl Price, Peter and Trisha Roselle and other leaders of prophetic intercession in the state of New Jersey at Liberty State Park, across the Hudson River from Manhattan and in view of the Statue of Liberty. Millions of immigrants who arrived on the East Coast stopped first at Ellis Island to document their desire to be part of this nation. Many of them headed to the historic train station at Liberty State Park to catch a train that would take them to Newark or New York City. We gathered at this train station to "open the gates in 2008" for the glory of God to flood across America.

Even before the meeting started, I could feel the Spirit of God moving, but when worship began, the Spirit of God fell on me. I was caught up into a heavenly place, and I received a vision that stretched from the past into the future. God is not in time; therefore He can communicate to us outside of the time period we are in. He can open the eyes of the spirit man to be able to see in a time that has not yet manifested, like He did for Daniel, Jeremiah and many of the biblical prophets. Apostles like John saw the time you and I are now living in and warned us of things to come. The Spirit of God lifts us into other realms so we can have hope and strategy for the future.

In the vision, which lasted for four hours, I saw both demonic and divine strategies, historical and future paths, and small groups and nations. In the next sections, I will explain what the Lord showed me and what I believe it means for us.

He Began with Me

The first thing the Lord showed me was my own bloodline. I already knew some of the history of my bloodline—the history of four generations on both sides of my family tree, and further back on my mother's side. The Lord showed me where the paths of my families intersected. He showed me where His Glory invaded our bloodline and also where demons had invaded and iniquitous structures had developed. I saw the progress Pam and I had made in overturning generational iniquities. But then He took me three years ahead and revealed the strategy of hell over two of my children. I saw how Satan would attempt to destroy them over the next several years. The Lord said, *Pray now! Gain authority over the enemy's plans!*

The Next Move Revealed

As worship continued, my spirit began to rise, as often happens during worship: We ascend high enough to have clear vision. Eventually, I could see the entire United States. The view was amazing, perplexing and confounding! I was caught between old and new paradigms and seasons of rule.

First, He revealed His remnant, showing me where they were positioned. Next, He showed me their strength from state to state. He then invaded time and showed me the future, seven years ahead. Troops began to assemble from every place in each state, as though they were drawn by a powerful magnet, and gathered to form what looked like a river of glory fire.

"Who are these people, Lord?" I asked, and He said, *This is My triumphant reserve for the future!* On that day I was looking into the future to see what would become a new movement. His triumphant reserve would be called up for future Kingdom purposes. This was the new wineskin and the movement that resulted from it.

A Resistance Began

When He began to gather His new reserve, I could see many were *not* attracted by this new movement. They refused to leave their religious structures, resisting His pull—His "magnet" of the new. They remained steadfast in old places of worship and religious rule that had become comfortable. I could hear sounds of the future that were creating a new move of His Spirit in the earth, but this group seemed deaf to it.

Throughout the Word of God, we find resistance to the new government or wineskin that God has ordained to rule in the future. In 2 Samuel 2:11; 3:1, we find this: "And the time that David was king in Hebron over the house of Judah was seven years and six months. . . . Now there was a long war between the house of Saul and the house of David." Let me clarify this Scripture. A Saul structure is not interested in establishing the glory of God in the future. The primary call to a Davidic structure, on the other hand, is movement of the Ark so that the Tabernacle that houses God's glory can be established. The war is really over the glory of God, not natural kingdom rule. You can form a new wineskin by initiating something that has never been; most wineskins, however, form like what you see in 2 Samuel—by shifting from one structure to another. It takes approximately seven years to redevelop the rule that will produce a better quality of life for the future.

Even as those who clung to religious structures resisted the new move of God, He showed me others aligning around race and sex instead of a mission call and gifting. Conflicts arose from this group, and I saw riots, lawlessness, prayerlessness and striving. This was similar to the vision God showed me in 1986, which I wrote about in chapter 1 and in *The Future War of the Church*. What stands out now is that even then God's people were triumphing. The vision was filled with victory.

The Triumphant People Arising

The movement of God's people—the river of glory fire— looked like liquid gold flowing in the land. It resembled fiery lava moving from state to state (every state had a movement). This group would destroy the works of the enemy in days ahead. Over the next seven years, they would mature to be ready to go to war against the darkness attempting to bring destruction.

Triumphant people are ones who know how to triumph. To *triumph* is to obtain victory, or a state of being victorious in conquest. Triumph carries a distinct emotion for God's children; in triumph, one expresses joy or exultation because he or she has prospered, succeeded and flourished. An easy way to understand triumph is to think of a card played that takes all others ("trumping," or winning a hand or suit). The triumphant people I saw had the following characteristics:

- **They were infused with a victorious attitude.** Attitudes—which signal the underlying emotions we have toward the tasks the Lord has given us—have a tremendous impact on how we see the world. Wrong attitudes can skew our perceptions and cloud our understanding of the fruits our labors are producing. Positioning your heart and mind on the Lord, however, will preserve you in times of trouble and lead to a victorious attitude. The Lord's triumphant people had strong hearts! Ask the Lord to adjust your attitude to triumph.

- **They were aligned for victory.** Attitude is linked with posture. Posture is linked with alignment. Posture and attitude, therefore, are linked with your positioning. An army must be aligned and ordered for victory. Alignment can be thought of as "snapping into place," the way a doctor must position a broken bone in its proper place in order for it to heal properly and the appendage to work again. God has an order, and it will not manifest until we are properly aligned. The triumphant people were snapped into alignment for victory. To create the prototype of triumph for the future, we must be aligned in God's order: first apostles, second prophets, third teachers, then healers, miracle workers, administrators, etc. Review your present alignments.

- **They occupied a high-level aptitude to adjust quickly.** Adapting to the needs of battle and adjusting to overcome the strategies of the enemy require aptitude. A quick ability to apprehend something is not actually dependent on your intelligence but on your attitude. Those of lesser intelligence can have the highest aptitude, and those who should have high aptitude can be sabotaged by their shoddy attitudes or lack of commitment to being aligned. We have to have an attitude that enables us to adjust quickly against our enemy and toward God's order. That attitude and resulting alignment allows you to see as God sees, both the parts and how they fit together as a whole. Then, like a machine, all components are fit together exactly, allowing it to function.

• **They were creative, cunning (more shrewd than the enemy) and confrontational.** Creativity and cunning are like weapons the Lord has given us to elude and overpower our enemy. But to use them effectively, we have to be willing to *confront* the enemy, whether we want to or not. Consider how Jesus, led by the Spirit, confronted Satan in the wilderness: It was the bringing together of two opposing forces in which truth could be revealed through God's Word and prevail.

In such confrontations, our creativity and cunning will give us the advantage. We will create the new from nothing. We will transform things into more prosperous forms or combine old forms into something with new qualities. And, though many Christians do not understand they are shrewder than the powers of darkness, we will outwit the enemy by our cunning, because our covenant relationship with God allows us to. We will make strategic moves at the right time to stay ahead of the enemy, as David did when King Saul pursued him (see 1 Samuel 18:11).

151

High Places and Ruling Demonic Centers

When He lifted me up, the Lord showed me the high places erected by the enemy in the United States. These are the result of the worship war going on in each territory of the earth. As stated previously, worship occurs around the one whose throne has been established. We are made to worship; therefore, if we pay homage to the enemy, he will control the atmosphere. The entire territory then falls under the darkness of his presence. Demonic hosts redirect those in that territory away from God's plan of fullness, peace, joy and abundance.

This is what I saw around the high places in each state, which had developed over years through idolatrous worship and wrong sacrifices. High places are actually worship altars. These altars had been built by the enemy and positioned strategically throughout the land. I saw how sacrifices on these altars empowered ruling hosts and held the atmosphere captive to them. This rule affected the entire atmosphere of the nation.

I could also see the atmosphere itself. In fact, I could even see different layers of the presence in the atmosphere. A war raged in each atmosphere. I could see the war between demonic hosts that were controlling the presence in the atmosphere and the glory of God trying to penetrate it. Some areas, already taken over, were ruled by darkness.

The enemy had already developed ten strategically positioned ruling centers throughout the United States. These were communication centers that transmitted to lesser substations from state to state. Then the Lord showed me the communication systems between these centers. When a sacrifice empowered one dimension of an evil presence, that presence would communicate with another center as they built their network and established their plan of control. While I believe it would be unwise to share everything I saw, I can say that there was a great relationship between political rule and mammon.

Covenant Roots in America

Throughout the history of the United States, individuals have established a covenant with the Holy One, leading to the formation of a *covenant root* in many territories. Because of this, a covenant war is occurring in the earth realm. (I will explain more about this in the next chapter.)

The Lord showed me the covenant roots that He has in the United States. I saw, further back, the covenant root that He had developed from Abraham's obedience. Devoted individuals or groups in America had been grafted into Abraham through their relationships with Jesus of Nazareth; they had in turn planted the spiritual root of Abraham into America's soil. Their lives were devoted to the Lord, and they came to this nation to gain spiritual freedom. Therefore, they made covenant between God and their new land. The inheritance of that covenant was then passed on through their descendants and spread into all of America.

This root of covenant grace had brought great life and prosperity to and from this land, but lifelines from the root system had withered. A great pruning was needed in the outer vines of this system. Actually, lifelines in parts of this nation had dried up, which changed the root structures in those places. Portions of New England, for example, had lost their power alignment, resulting in the formation of corrupted root structures.

The Lord showed me some roots covered by a mossy, evil slime that could still be removed. He showed me states that had never allowed a covenant root to go down into their land. He showed me broken covenants that would have to be mended before roots could grow fruit in the future.

My wife, who worked in horticulture at Texas A&M and is a certified master gardener, wrote the following to help me understand the withering root of fruit that I saw from heaven:

Several years ago, I read an article in a Christian magazine comparing viruses to sin. Viruses can invade, weaken and debilitate a person. After experiencing barrenness for ten years, being healed and becoming pregnant with our first child, I was invaded by three of the five TORCH syndrome viruses. Just one of these viruses can deform the fetus. God, in His grace and love, protected both Rebekah Faith, who was in my womb, and me, and we miraculously overcame the attack. My Catholic doctor wept when the child was born healthy. I had to learn much from this circumstance.

I love gardening generally, but God's presence is especially strong in the Israel Prayer Garden here at Global Spheres Center. My recent encounter with a particularly nasty virus affecting roses in the prayer garden has reminded me of the similarities between viral infections and the insidious effects of sin. I feel it is important for each of us as we walk through the narrow places that we are presently maneuvering.

Rose rosette disease is caused by a virus spread by a tiny mite. This wingless mite travels passively on the wind and transmits the disease to the nonnative (and quite invasive) multiflora rose, as well as to cultivated garden roses. Also known as the "witches' broom of rose," this virus has no proven treatment, even though there are recommended steps for dealing with it—steps ranging from hope-infused organic treatments to ripping the affected plant out of the garden and discarding it in the Dumpster!

In roses infected with the disease, the leaves become deformed, crinkled and brittle. As the disease progresses, leaves become very small, petioles are shortened, and most lateral buds begin producing short, intensely red shoots. In cultivated roses, symptoms include thickened stems and a proliferation of thorns. The disease weakens the plant significantly and makes it more susceptible to freeze damage. Small plants are usually killed in about two years, while a large plant may survive for five years in a deteriorated condition.

My first introduction to rose rosette involved a lovely climbing white rose in the Israel Prayer Garden two years ago. At the first sign of symptoms, I pruned the affected branch down to the base of the plant and used a series of organic treatments. Then I waited. The following spring, the new growth on the rose again produced the twisted witches' broom deformities. When that happened, I followed the more drastic step and condemned the entire plant to the dumpster.

Since that first encounter, we have diligently watched for signs of rose rosette disease throughout the Global Spheres Center grounds. To date, we have removed five other roses that did not respond to treatment. During that same time, we have also taken authority over the disease and seen roses rebound, prosper and blossom.

Through this experience, I have seen two seemingly dichotomous principles at work: the principle of faith overcoming disease and destruction and the principle of, "If your right hand offends you, cut it off"! This is where a more thorough understanding of the viral mechanism comes in handy.

In rose rosette disease, the mite introduces the virus into a branch of the rose plant. The virus then works its way into the vascular system of the plant and travels down to the crown, or base. From there, the virus can travel into other branches of the plant, infecting the entire rose. If the gardener is vigilant and cuts out the offending branch before the infection travels to the plant's center, the rose may avoid further infection and live on in health and prosperity. If the gardener is unobservant or overworked, however, he or she might miss the telltale signs of the virus and lose valuable time, thus allowing the virus to gain a foothold and overtake the plant.

Our experience with this virus has shown us that vigilance can only go so far. Often sin finds an inroad, plants a seed of corruption and overtakes an organism. When that happens and we are too late to cut out the offending branch, we must throw ourselves upon the mercy of a loving, compassionate Father who longs to see us healed and set free from the sin that so easily besets us. Isaiah 61:1–3 (emphasis mine) says this:

> The Spirit of the Lord GOD is upon Me, because the LORD has anointed Me to preach good tidings to the poor; He has sent Me to heal the brokenhearted, to proclaim liberty to the captives, and the opening of the prison to those who are bound; to proclaim the acceptable year of the LORD, and the day of vengeance of our God; to comfort all who mourn, to console those who mourn in Zion, to give them beauty for ashes, the oil of joy for mourning, the garment of praise for the spirit of heaviness; that they may be called trees of righteousness, the *planting* of the LORD, that He may be glorified.

The witches' broom of rose is a great example of a root being bewitched! Galatians 5:7, 9 says, "You ran well. Who hindered you from obeying the truth? . . . A little leaven leavens the whole lump." *One* airborne mite can infect a whole plant.

Witchcraft actually sends a word with a person's name through the air to produce a wrong thought or control pattern in a person, thus capturing his or her freedom to worship. One word, thought or action that enters a person's thinking can cause decay to begin. This is a time to capture all of our thoughts, as Paul wrote in 2 Corinthians 10:4–6, and become new vessels of freedom and liberty. What Pam endeavored to do in the garden is a perfect example of the vigilance that has to occur in a remnant people to change the course of an infected land and atmosphere. It is the only way a new fragrance of His glory will invade the land of covenant called America. *This is a season of pruning and uprooting.*

After I saw the covenant roots and the corrupted roots in America, the Lord revealed conflicts between the root systems. Over the next several years, these conflicts will determine what sort of fruit will be brought forth in America. The conflicts will multiply and intensify—I actually saw "orchards of contention." The interesting thing is that different people groups in each orchard created a different type of fruit, which had not been tasted in past seasons. I related this biblically to the church that came out of Antioch, because it was an international church that came about for Kingdom advancement in that season in history.

Whose Voice Will Be Heard?

Next, the Lord showed me how the communication system in the United States was linked with systems internationally, and the beginning of a new form of global communication in the demonic realm. This communication controlled financial and legal structures, which had a ruling voice set against the God of Israel. Therefore, I knew that during the next seven years, beginning in 2008, Israel would experience much warfare. This was interesting, since I sent my son Daniel, his wife and my grandchildren to live there during this time, during which they have lived through two wars in that land.

Financial and legal structures were manipulated through the insurance system, led by America, which was used to disqualify many from being established in key places that would prosper them in the future by recording their weaknesses and movements. This was similar to what happened in the days of the Nazi regime.

I saw a war in heaven over these communication centers. Seven major obelisks served as towers of communication, located in Luxor, Egypt; Rome; Istanbul; Paris; Buenos Aires; Washington, D.C.; and Las Vegas. A host of other obelisk structures spread over the earth. When religious false communication was released, the words bounced from obelisk to obelisk. The cities of the major obelisks contended for control. (Constantine actually requested that an Egyptian obelisk be shipped to Constantinople to empower religious government rule. This will always cause the Church to be subservient to the rule of a nation's government.)

Freedom Outposts Become Apostolic Centers

The Lord also showed me, however, His buildings where the remnant would gather, network and communicate. He Himself was erecting these and forming them for a time in the future. (Though I was in 2008, I could see these places in 2015–2016.)

These centers looked like fiery, vibrant castles strategically developed and placed in the earth. Not every state had one. I asked the Lord what these were, and He said, *These are My freedom outposts for the future.* When His triumphant reserve connected with the centers, they went in one way and came out seven times brighter and stronger.

I saw 23 states in America with covenant roots. Many states had freedom outposts, but He showed me where others were needed. Where the spiritual atmosphere was not yet conducive to freedom, He showed me how outposts could begin to form, changing the atmosphere and the land. Inside them I could hear sounds and see new types of warfare that will have to be developed by the triumphant people to regain new portions of the lands where they are located. I saw that prayer strategies from the last season will not be effective in the next. Nazareth and Capernaum are examples of this in Jesus' day. I thought of how the Lord told the disciples, "These will not come out except through prayer and fasting."

I now believe that He was showing me the apostolic centers I mentioned in chapter 3, which are forming for a shift in a worship war in the earth realm.[3] An apostolic center is not a mega-church. When the triumphant reserve reached one of these centers, their very cells were drastically empowered by the indwelling glory of God. They were re-empowered to do the works of Jesus at an accelerated rate.

The Nations Are the Lord's

The Lord showed me 153 sheep nations that would align with Israel for the future. They looked like fish moving in water. Later, as I was reading the book of John, I happened on this verse:

> When they went ashore, they saw a fire with a fish lying on the coals, and they saw a loaf of bread. Jesus told them, "Bring some of the fish you've just caught." Simon Peter got into the boat and pulled the net ashore. Though the net was filled with 153 large fish, it was not torn. Jesus told them, "Come, have breakfast." None of the disciples dared to ask him who he was. They knew he was the Lord. Jesus took the bread, gave it to them, and did the same with the fish. This was the third time that Jesus showed himself to the disciples after he had come back to life.
>
> John 21:9–14 GW

The context of this verse is the return of the Lord after the resurrection and before the ascension. His disciples had returned to their normal way of life—fishing—and were toiling in the old structure that supplied their daily needs. This is where He had met them early on, and this is where they returned to be met by Him again. But Jesus was extending a call to them; in verse 6, He showed a specific way to prosper for the future: "Throw the net out on the right side of the boat."

I teach frequently on the brain and our ways of thinking. Because the right brain is creative, I had always viewed this passage as revealing a new, creative way of prospering. Now, however, I saw it from a different perspective.

When Jesus had prepared the fire, the disciples counted 153 fish in their net. I saw these as the nations of the "third day." (You can read more about the Third Day Church in *The Future War of the Church*.) These "fish" or "sheep" nations would be used to break open the new day in the earth. In the vision, I could see them clearly.

Though the Lord showed me the United States of America in detail, I could see that each nation aligned with the pattern shown in the vision: a triumphant reserve, a movement, a covenant war with contending thrones, a communication system of both good and evil, and the Lord calling for the apostolic Church to arise and new centers of glory to form.

New Calls for a New Season

The Lord then showed me new calls extended from heaven and angels bringing those calls to the earth. The intercession and travail of today are opening the gates of heaven, so that these calls will reach the appropriate ones to lead in this hour.

Finally, I saw His new leadership, one not just of the young generation but of realigned generations. Three generations were aligned to bring forth David's mighty army. When they aligned, their hearts became one with His, and the strength to overcome was released.

As this book comes to a close, I will explain the process of triumph, fullness and presence. Let's look first, however, at the covenant wars in days ahead.

7

Overcomers of the Covenant War

All warfare that we enter into is centered around the covenant of which we are a part. We must always remember that, through a covenant, God offered Abraham a land of promise. In our hearts, I believe we are always seeking to find our land of covenant. We are never really satisfied until we are established in the place God has for our faith to touch Him.

One of my favorite movies as a child was *The Wizard of Oz*, a story of desire for a land of promise "somewhere over the rainbow." Dorothy, the lead character, attempts to define her future apart from her family farm in Kansas, and she goes off in search of perfection. But she encounters far more warfare than she was experiencing in humdrum Kansas. From the time she reaches her "Promised Land," it begins—in the midst of her beautiful new surroundings, she discovers she has accidently dethroned one ruling force and must contend with another. The further she presses toward Oz, the capital of this utopian land, the more she must confront.

There are lessons to be learned here. One is that your promise is all around you, if you will just open your eyes to see! To occupy and establish your promise, however, you encounter great warfare, because warfare always comes with anything worth acquiring. You must not simply long to occupy some place you think will be perfect. Rather, there is a call to war for the blessings of any land worth occupying.

One line from *The Wizard of Oz* influences the way I think about most things: "Lions and tigers and bears—oh my!" In the Bible you find "Egyptians and giants and Pharisees—oh my!" In the world you are confronted with "poverty and infirmity and religion (all kinds)—oh my!"

You can sum up the war of the nations with "Israel (and the Middle East) and Russia and China—oh my!" Notice that America is not in this lineup: By 2026, there will be a new alignment of nations in the earth. The battlefields of the world are being defined. Who will rule in these fields will be determined by the nations clustering around the three listed above. America will be more aligned with China than Russia or Israel.

A Shaking Is Coming

In the years ahead the nations will experience what is written in the book of Hebrews and prophesied by Haggai: There will be a shaking! Shaking unlocks a new glory and favor. It produces wealth. It rearranges how nations are aligned. (In the next chapters, I will share what the shaking will look like.)

After returning from Babylon, reformation had begun in the land of Israel. Nehemiah had led God's people to rebuild the wall around Jerusalem, while Ezra had helped awaken them to their spiritual heritage. As the Word of God was read publicly, like a sunrise appearing after seventy long winters of storms, the people became aware of the covenant they had broken and abandoned (see Nehemiah 8). The grief from leaving God's covenant overwhelmed them until the instruction of the covenant revealed that the "joy of the LORD" would release the strength necessary to continue their reformation process (verse 10). The ultimate goal was the restoration of worship.

For worship to be restored, the Temple had to be rebuilt. The warfare that goes with reformation, however, intensified when this happened. The people grew disillusioned, disinterested and, eventually, despondent. Instead of pressing to build the place that would restore their centrality of worship and re-create their identity as a people, they shifted from worship to self and built their own homes and businesses (see Haggai 1:2–4). The enemy's greatest resource is man's self and unsanctified desires. While building their own homes was necessary, once again they had shifted from God's blueprint of beginning with His house.

Seventeen years elapsed. God then raised up a prophet to decree His will. To get this stalled-out reformation moving again, Haggai began to prophesy,

> For thus says the Lord of hosts: Yet once more, in a little while, I will shake and make tremble the [starry] heavens, the earth, the sea, and the dry land; and I will shake all nations and the desire and the precious things of all nations

shall come in, and I will fill this house with splendor, says
the Lord of hosts.

Haggai 2:6–7 AMPC

Shaking must occur to reorder God's will in the earth; this
would become the pattern for ages to come, as Hebrews
12:6, 25–28 (AMPC) says:

For the Lord corrects and disciplines everyone whom He
loves, and He punishes, even scourges, every son whom He
accepts and welcomes to His heart and cherishes. . . . So see
to it that you do not reject Him or refuse to listen to and heed
Him Who is speaking [to you now]. For if they [the Israelites]
did not escape when they refused to listen and heed Him Who
warned and divinely instructed them [here] on earth [reveal-
ing with heavenly warnings His will], how much less shall we
escape if we reject and turn our backs on Him Who cautions
and admonishes [us] from heaven? Then [at Mount Sinai]
His voice shook the earth, but now He has given a promise:
Yet once more I will shake and make tremble not only the
earth but also the [starry] heavens. Now this expression, Yet
once more, indicates the final removal and transformation
of all [that can be] shaken—that is, of that which has been
created—in order that what cannot be shaken may remain
and continue. [See Psalm 102:26.] Let us therefore, receiving a kingdom that is firm and stable and cannot be shaken,
offer to God pleasing service and acceptable worship, with
modesty and pious care and godly fear and awe.

The world will be contended for by nations whose roots
are still aligned with Babel. The earth is the Lord's, however,
and the fullness thereof! The one determining force that is
not listed among these nations is the triumphant reserve of
the apostolic Church that is rising. God has a Kingdom of

people, a nation above all nations. These people hold the "trump card" of influence over the world, the flesh and the devil—*oh my*! Built within God's children is His covenant authority to be used in a timely manner. When we exercise God's authority within us, we will overtake every plan of the enemy and release a strategy of fullness in the earth.

The War of the Generations

The authority we gain with covenant is released in the context of *family*. Because I experienced the blessing of family and its subsequent loss and destruction, the family unit is precious to my heart and fuels my drive for freedom. I enjoy the uniqueness of each of my children. I love training them in the way *they* should go: I watch and listen to their desires and try to influence their choices as much as any dad would without controlling them. I feel the same about the Body of Christ. I long to see each member equipped and operating in his or her gift. My greatest role and service to both my family and God's people is teaching them how to war against their enemy—not as individuals warring against a shrewd foe, but warring collectively to overcome him.

Family units should be war units. The first war unit in the earth was to be family. God's will is to back the families of earth that represent Him. In the shaking that is coming, however, family and ministry relations will also be shaken. God's covenant is the focal point of all warfare; the entire Bible is a record of God's aligned covenant being (or not being) expressed. At the beginning, man did well in the garden God set up for him, but after he listened to the serpent and aligned with his will, the garden shifted, and mankind had to shift. God's quest to find someone to realign His covenant plan brought Him to Abraham, and His family became the recipient of God's covenant.

The prophets all addressed covenant with God, family and Israel. Joel prophesied a restoration between God and man that would cause our sons and daughters to prophesy. Zechariah prophesied that boys and girls would once again play in the streets protected from violence. Malachi concludes the writings of the initial covenant between God and man with a prophetic decree for reconciliation between fathers and sons. Elijah would be sent again to turn the hearts of estranged fathers (and mothers) to ungodly and rebellious children, bringing repentance and realigning and reconciling one with the other—thus lifting the effects of curses off the land.

Understanding family and corporate spiritual gatherings and gaining strategy for war are important concepts for our future. The greatest relationships in the ancient Mediterranean world were not limited to the husband-wife relationship but included the interrelations of siblings. This is how the concept of tribe developed. The family/tribe produced the army. That eventually produced nations.

This concept of gaining strategy for war through family is still valid. There is a reason that, after having led the Israelites into the Promised Land, Joshua had one message for them: Choose you this day whom you will serve (see Joshua 24:15). The apostolic government leader who had been chosen by the Lord to establish the people also represented the people in forming a covenant with the Lord, which was an updated version of the Sinai covenant. God has created mankind in such a way that we must activate our will by choosing His will. If we do this, we prosper; if not, there are eventual consequences.

I believe the choice of a family to be righteous in the earth can save a generation and prolong the Spirit of God's presence in the earth realm. Noah gained favor and chose for his family. "As in the days of Noah" is now!

Family to Body of Christ to Army

In the New Testament the concept of gathering was shifted from the tribe to the church, or *ekklesia*. Therefore, we find a relationship of church to family. Family, tribe, church gathering and the Body of Christ (a nation above all nations) are key relationships for us to understand as we go to war in the future.

In the Hebraic culture, families warred together and prospered together; then their prosperity was passed from one generation to another. A mindset of preservation and posterity developed. In American society, people do not have the same concern for preservation of one generation's estate so that it may be passed on to the next.

Writing about Mediterranean attitudes toward family in his book *The Ancient Church as Family*, Joseph Hellerman shares,

> Augmenting—at times even supplanting—attention to present family relationships is a preoccupation with the past and the future of the patrilineal kin group. Future orientation revolves around making arrangements for the proper distribution of family inheritance. At work in each case is the descent group view of the family as a corporation that takes priority over, and survives the demise of, its individual members. Both the constant appeal to family ancestry and the preoccupation with inheritance reflect the broader concern for the survival of the kin group and the retention of the family's honor. . . . [The] tightest unit of loyalty and affection is the descent group of brothers and sisters. The emotional bonding characteristic

of marriage in *Western* families is normally a mark of sibling (or mother-son) relationships.[1] [Emphasis added.]

Relational failure is epitomized in the betrayal of a sibling—think about Cain and Abel, or Jacob and Esau, or Joseph and his brothers. The church is to be a family with sibling relationships, such that biblical writers felt the Church should operate as an economic family unit. In contrast, in the West we find "no convictions that one's value as an individual is contingent upon the honor or achievements of one's ancestor(s). Inheritance [is] understood individually: each child is entitled to his or her share."[2] This contrasts with the Hebraic belief that "personal honor is strongly dependent on one's ancestral lineage."[3]

In ancient Mediterranean society, siblings reflected what we think of as a healthy husband-wife relationship. Today, the greatest war has been the invasion of the enemy into family life. Dysfunctional family life has been one of the greatest detriments to understanding the concept of overcoming in war. Divorce and covenant breaking have created a root of disloyalty and lack of honor in regard to the family. In the Biblical understanding of war, siblings shared responsibility for protection of family honor from invading outsiders. When they overcame invaders, they could share the spoils of the battle. Hellerman summarizes this by saying, "When it comes to choosing sides, brother must side with brothers regardless of the issue at hand."[4]

Here are some values at the heart of Mediterranean conviction about sibling relationships:

- If an enemy invaded the family and harmed someone, the other family members would arise and bring retribution as quickly as possible.

- Family members were discreet with the issues of other members to preserve family honor. This could also become a fault if family honor was preserved at the cost of truth.
- Family members were expected to share their material resources, including clothing, shelter, food and military power and strength.

Undercover counterintelligence teams on impossible missions to overthrow covert operations of the enemy call themselves family. Many sports teams working together to win a championship call themselves family. Police units band together and call themselves family. Even the Mafia are called family. The concept of a single person being wholly devoted to a group and its mission is family. Jesus and His disciples became family, and the early Church had a family mentality that has dissipated in modern society. Instead of embracing the call to covenant and understanding the strength of corporate wholeness, we live in a world of covenant separation.

The Origins of Covenant

All warfare in the earthly realm, whether spiritual or natural, is an outgrowth of God's covenant plan of fullness for the earth and man's role in accomplishing this purpose. The enemies of God's covenant create war against those who strive to represent His covenant in the earth. I believe if we understand God's covenant, then we will understand the warfare around us. All discipline we go through as children of God is a result of His love for us so that we experience all the promises of His covenant. God longs to have a covenant with you personally, corporately, territorially and generationally. Victory over all of your enemies is assured once you are in covenant with the Lord.

What is covenant? Covenant is an endless partnership or solemn and binding agreement between two or more parties. Covenant with God establishes a commitment to a relationship that allows His purpose for us to be fulfilled. In their book *The Covenants*, Kevin Conner and Ken Malmin explain that covenant

> has lost its meaning and significance in present society. In Bible times, the word "covenant" involved promise, commitment, faithfulness and loyalty even unto death. A covenant was sacred and was not lightly entered into by the parties involved. In Bible times, a person was only as good as their covenant word. In a society where national agreements, business contracts and marriage covenants are under stress and attack, where people are "covenant-breakers" (Romans 1:31), it brings great joy and comfort to know that God is a covenant-making and covenant-keeping God.[5]

Covenant with God is always initiated by God Himself. We cannot manipulate God in this respect. We cannot go to Him and say, "Here's our proposal; You agree with what we want to accomplish." God sets the boundaries of His agreement in the earth realm. We are responsible to operate within those boundaries.

We can clearly see the covenant pattern throughout the Bible, from creation through redemption. Even before the Fall, God expressed His purpose for humanity in the Edenic covenant, through which God planted a garden with established boundaries. The promises that lay therein contain God's purpose for creating the human race: being made in

God's image, fruitfulness, multiplication, subduing the earth and having dominion.

God created man so man could come into agreement with Him and to communicate His will so man could become "the keepers of His earth." When Adam and Eve broke the conditions of the covenant, their disobedience necessitated an expression of God's redemptive purpose for the human race in the form of redemptive covenants. In God's desire to align with man, we see a progression that includes some unsuccessful attempts, including the Adamic (Genesis 3) and the Noahic (Genesis 6–9) covenants.

The Warfare to Form Covenant

These attempts never came to fullness because of man's shortcomings. Hence, God's search continued. The warfare over covenant is a result of an intermediary, anti-God force that does not want God and man in alignment, and it has always been intense. In the beginning, God's covenant with man was a product of boundaries, communication and allegiance. His ultimate will was that the Garden of Eden, where man communed with Him and experienced His glory, would spread. In the end, the war will be the same. Will mankind commune with God through His Son, the Lord Jesus Christ, to release glory in the earth realm?

One of my favorite sayings is, "But God!" He is determined to align us with all that He has planned for us. Therefore, God's pursuit of man includes a covenant that will produce the fullness of His plan in the earth.

Let's look at the blessings, promises and warfare of this pursuit through covenant, as seen in the following covenant alignments:

- Abrahamic (Genesis 12–22)
- Mosaic (Exodus 19–40; Galatians 3:24)
- Israelite (Deuteronomy 27–33)
- Davidic (2 Samuel 7; Psalm 89; 132)
- New Covenant (Jeremiah 31:31–34; Hebrews 8–9; Matthew 26)

The everlasting covenant, the final expression between God and man, is the most comprehensive expression of both God's creative and redemptive purposes for humanity. This included a Messiah who could redeem the losses that had occurred in the progression of the other covenants. Though man failed in keeping the garden, God promised that we would have ultimate victory over our enemy, the devil! (See Genesis 3:15.)

This promise of ultimate victory was part of the promise released to Adam and Eve when their violation of boundaries disrupted their communion established by the covenant of the garden. Their sons warred over worship and firstfruits giving, resulting in the land crying out for reconciliation. Cain drifted and wandered because of lost covenant. The further mankind drifts from our prescribed boundaries and God's order of worship, the more evil we become.

Ultimately man found himself in a terrible warfare described "as in the days of Noah." God's response led to the first use of the word *covenant* in the Bible, in Genesis 6:18. The people of Noah's day had strayed so deeply into sin and away from God's plan for the earth that God finally had to supernaturally start over by releasing a new agreement with the earth. The agreement came through Noah, a man God knew He could trust with His plan. Noah's very name meant "rest," a prophetic sign of the rest God wanted to bring from sin and its consequent curse that prevailed in those days. Noah was dedicated to the Lord, so when the Lord spoke to him, Noah began the process of restoring the earth back into relationship with a Holy God. The covenant God forged with Noah has affected every generation since.

This process of restoration was realized in the earth time and again. Man drifted from God's covenant purposes and experienced His discipline; because of Noah's obedience, however, we know that we have providential care! This was God's promise to Noah (Genesis 8:21–9:17): Though mankind might grow wicked, God would not ultimately destroy us. There was a redemptive plan of recovery. In Genesis 9:8–11, God gave a covenantal promise that a flood would never again destroy the whole earth. Then He gave the rainbow as a sign to remind people of His power, so that when they saw it, they would remember His agreement with the earth.

We can conclude that *even in the midst of us violating our relationship with the Lord, He is always ready to redeem and add a new level of His promise and will into our ultimate destiny.* That is the God we serve. When we fail, He disciplines us over our present lack of agreement with Him, and then He adds another incredible promise that He longs for us to experience. Our failures do not stop His future plans for fullness.

God has not called us to be sweet, frail, harmless followers. We are fiery worship warriors who will not stop our pursuit of God until we lay hold of His ultimate plan—"the earth is the Lord's and the fullness thereof." We triumph!

Abraham, the Example of Covenant Alignment

Abraham will always be preeminent, for an inheritance (son), a land (Canaan), those who aligned with him and all nations of the earth could find blessing in him. The call to Abraham (Abram in the beginning) was a new birth: The initiation of relationship with him dramatically changed the spiritual nature of mankind. God planned from the beginning for all humans to fulfill His divine mission; His heart is for all to align themselves with Him, through Torah and by His Son. We think Torah is limited to the first five books of the Bible, but actually the word just means the teachings of God. Torah was extended through the teaching of the Lord Jesus Christ as He walked in the earth and represented the Father. Where Adam and Noah failed, Abraham earned the right to align with a Holy God and thus be the plumb line for all mankind. To do this, he endured great testing.

The Tests of Covenant

Many of us never get past our personal warfare; therefore, we are not called to the corporate wars for territories and generations. Abraham did not receive this incredible call by default, but rather by withstanding all the tests included in the great benefits of knowing God. He endured ten of them to become fully aligned with God and to gain access to heaven's promises in the earth realm.

God knows all future events of mankind, but trials are meant to display to the world how much we love God and are willing to obey Him. They also qualify us for a call, identity and authority to rule over the enemy and his plan in the earth. The Lord would not test you without you knowing that you are capable of overcoming these tests. God does not impose trials beyond our capacity. God tests you because He knows you are capable of exerting His righteous rule in a situation—for example, Psalm 105:19 conveys that "the word of the LORD tested him" (Joseph).

The person being tested has a free choice to withstand the tests or submit to the ruling force in it. James 4:7 (AMPC) instructs us to "be subject to God. Resist the devil [stand firm against him], and he will flee from you." Once we do this, our potential becomes strength and action—we move from our capabilities into a relationship in which the very strength of God flows through us and we triumph.

Abraham faced the following ten tests before fully passing his mantle to a new generation. This list is paralleled throughout Scripture, in both the Old and New Covenants; you will find these tests in Elisha's life and see Jesus instructing His disciples using them (Luke 14).

1. Leave your land and family . . . for your own benefit. Cutting ties, overcoming the emotional structure of familiarity and leaving earthly fatherly security and friends to receive the unknown promise of land and wealth is not an easy choice.

2. In midst of hard times, we must move with God. Abraham knew that, to overcome hunger and famine in Canaan (his promise), he must leave and find provision and refuge elsewhere.

3. Even in our call to follow God, we sometimes make unwise choices. Abraham's choice in Egypt resulted in Sarah's abduction. In our immature, fearful choices in life, the Lord still intervenes to protect us as long as we continue on our ultimate journey with Him. When Abraham shares a half-truth about his wife, God intervenes with the full truth.

4. Though we separate from relatives, we still have a responsibility to engage in warfare over their future destiny. When Lot is captured, Abraham engages in warfare

to retrieve him from the enemy. God never intends for us to negate our call to help those in our bloodline.

5. After assuming that Sarah would never give birth, Abraham cohabits with an outside resource, Hagar, to create a lineage.

6. At 99 years of age, Abraham must roll away the reproach of the past through the commandment of circumcision as a sign for all generations—a most painful test.

7. Once again, Abraham reveals his fear of loss and death by giving Sarah to Abimelech to protect himself.

8. To give up a tie with another soul is difficult. However, to appease the true line of covenant blessing, Abraham must allow Sarah to drive Hagar away while she was pregnant.

9. Years later, Abraham must give up his first son, Ishmael. To let go of any child is a difficult task.

10. After years of overcoming trials and barrenness, finally a child is born, leading to the greatest test of all: Abraham must give up his only son, Isaac, binding him on the altar and trusting God with the future. Isaac was the only way into the future. This was Abraham's ultimate test. The maturity he displayed after all the other tests proved he was worthy to be called a friend of God, one whom all others can align with in the future.

Abraham as Warrior

Most people think of Abraham as a father, patriarch and pioneer. His call as a military commander, however, is what opened the way for the Lord to make covenant with him. In his fourth test, Abraham and 318 of his servants pursued, defeated and plundered an army who had captured his nephew,

Lot (see Genesis 14). This was no band of pirates looting the countryside—it was Chedorlaomer, king of Elam of Mesopotamia, and three of his allies who sought to regain their control over the five cities of the Jordanian plain, including Sodom and Gomorrah.

After subjugating and plundering the Rephaimites, the Zuzimites, the Emimites, the Horites, the Amalekites and the Amorites, they finally attacked Sodom and Gomorrah, carrying off plunder and people (including Lot). When the news came to Abraham, he did not hesitate or fret. He gathered his men and pursued a large army of experienced fighting men.

In the Bible, Abraham's men were referred to as "trained servants" who must have been trained in more than just sheep herding. This aspect of Abraham is not often noted. Abraham was a warrior who trained his servants to be warriors. He lived in a dangerous time and traveled through hazardous territories. He was not the sweet, frail, harmless old gentleman that he is often imagined to be. He could take care of himself.

When Abraham caught up with the Mesopotamian kings, he did not just charge and hope to win; he had to devise a strategy that would enable his small band of men to overthrow a larger, well-equipped army. He divided his warriors into two groups, and at night, when the Mesopotamians slept with bellies full of food and wine, Abraham's warriors attacked. This was like a Delta Force movie! The Mesopotamian soldiers were thrown into confusion and scattered, and Abraham and his men chased them as far as Damascus. Abraham brought back the spoils and captives—including, of course, his nephew Lot.

This victory was the key to Abram crossing over into his future. It created a leadership alignment. Abraham had proven himself a warrior-leader worthy of following. Sodom, in his appreciation, offered a great reward. This peculiar victory and association with Sodom led Abraham to a key contact for his future: Melchizedek, king of Salem, the prophetic future site of the Temple of the Holy God. Though Abraham, as victor in the war, was entitled to all the spoils, he recognized the legality and legitimacy of the King of Salem. By doing this, he rejected personal gain from the war; instead he gave, and his giving unlocked his future.

Covenant Is Extended Yet Again

In this victory in warfare, God assured Abraham how to face his future, revealing Himself as a *shield of Abraham*. This meant that Abraham's future would never be extinguished. All people who align with him for their future will not be extinguished. The name that God revealed to Abraham included mercy and judgment. He assured Abraham that he would have offspring to carry forth all that God had promised. His offspring would also, by exercise of their faith, be assured that God would always back them.

From that moment, Abraham's trust of God and ability to place total confidence in Him seemed to shift. He began to trust God in a new way, and God considered this trust an act of righteousness. He then made a covenant with Abraham, and Abraham responded by making an offering to God. Through this blood sacrifice he was assured of his future. God then shared the boundaries of His promise and gave him the right to overtake every enemy within that boundary. These are keys to understanding our warfare: righteousness, boundaries and the ability to overtake our enemies.

This alignment becomes the plumb line for mankind and all nations for all generations to come. God formed Israel through Abraham's righteous alignment. He has a covenant with this land promised to Abraham; it is the prototype for all nations. All warfare in earth is set against this plumb line. When we war with this land and its boundaries, we war with the God of Abraham, also known as the God of Israel.

Abraham did not always appear to pass every test. He always trusted God to keep him moving forward on his journey, however, and never deviated from it. We "fail forward" into the best that God has for us.

Gaining the Everlasting Covenant

This covenant of Abraham has been made available because God the Father gave a sacrifice to all mankind. By giving His only Son as a redemptive act to redeem all mankind, each individual now has access to righteousness, or right standing with Him. We have a way to exchange our blood for His blood through His Spirit dwelling in us. This New Covenant exchanges animal sacrifices for grace. It will always eclipse every other covenant.

Connor and Malmin describe the benefits of the New Covenant as "forgiveness and remission of the penalty of sin, justification and righteousness, being born again into the family of God, assurance, sanctification to the Lord, adoption as sons and daughters of God and glorification."[6] We must learn to connect with what has paved the way for our freedom. In doing this we will have an advocate for victory. We are each capable of overcoming the forces and temptations that would prevent us from triumphing!

When the time came for Jesus to reveal His ultimate identity as redeemer of mankind, He, too, was tested. I call this "the great wilderness face-off." These tests were not internal; the purpose of temptation or testing is for one to gain advantage over another at the point of our inward, original intent or influence.

Satan had to tempt Jesus on two fronts: His identity as Messiah *and* man. These temptations assaulted His new vocation, call and mission and were meant to tempt Him as head of the new movement, not the old fallen race. They were to stop God's redemptive plan for mankind—to stop the power of the anointing that had come from heaven to break the yoke that mankind was wearing from past failures.

In His quest to overcome, Jesus became hungry. As Man, would He succumb to the flesh? Satan fully realized Jesus' famished condition, but Jesus knew He must deny all flesh so that only the Word could be exhibited as it was made flesh.

Attempting to plant doubt in Jesus' mind, Satan incited Him to dissatisfaction, impatience and self-will. Why should He deny Himself? Jesus' weapon in resisting this seduction was the Torah: He humbled Himself and quoted Deuteronomy 8:3, "Man shall not live by bread alone; but man lives by every word that proceeds from the mouth of the LORD." When Jesus used the Torah as a sword, the sword became life against the enemy and overcame his plan. This was the first trump card Jesus played.

Again the enemy played his own card, tempting Jesus based on His call. He will do the same to you. Since Jesus came to redeem the kingdoms of this world, the enemy offered the world to Jesus. But the offered gift came out of its proper time. Jesus used Deuteronomy 6:13 (AMPC) to counter him: "You shall [reverently] fear the Lord your God and serve Him and swear by His name [and presence]." Jesus did not compromise to gain dominion!

Finally, Jesus was tempted to put God to a test. This was the height of presumption. This time, Satan used the Word to justify the temptation, quoting its promise that angels would take charge over Jesus (Psalm 91:11–12). In return, Jesus used Deuteronomy 6:16 (AMPC), "You shall not tempt and try the Lord your God as you tempted and tried Him in Massah." The tempter was trumped again, as Jesus gained power to rebuke him and send him away for a time.

The Promise Extended

As we learn to play the trump card of the Word at the right time, we triumph. Our ultimate triumph, as Connor and Malmin write, will be manifested at the Second Coming of Christ:

> The promises of this ultimate covenant include everlasting life, immortality, an everlasting kingdom which the believer inherits, an everlasting inheritance, everlasting love, kindness and mercy, everlasting habitations, everlasting joy, everlasting strength and an everlasting name.
>
> Additionally, overcomers can lay claim to . . . receiving the eternal tree of life, freedom from hurt by death, hidden manna and a white stone with a new name on it, power over the nations, ruling and reigning with Jesus over all enemies, being clothed with a white raiment of light and having their names confessed before the Father and the angels, being a pillar in the Temple of God, sitting with Jesus on His throne, and inheriting all things.[7]

What amazing promises for us to grasp!

In my own life, the Lord helped me grasp these covenant promises and my responsibility within them by reading John 14–17. Much of God's covenant relationship with us, both present and to come, is revealed through such verses as these:

Most assuredly, I say to you, he who believes in Me, the works that I do he will do also; and greater works than these he will do, because I go to My Father. And whatever you ask in My name, that I will do, that the Father may be glorified in the Son. If you ask anything in My name, I will do it. If you love Me, keep My commandments. And I will pray the Father, and He will give you another Helper, that He may abide with you forever.

John 14:12–16

You did not choose Me, but I chose you and appointed you that you should go and bear fruit, and that your fruit should remain, that whatever you ask the Father in My name He may give you.

John 15:16

These things I have spoken to you, that in Me you may have peace. In the world you will have tribulation; but be of good cheer, I have overcome the world.

Luke 16:33

And for their sakes I sanctify Myself, that they also may be sanctified by the truth.

Luke 17:19

Those who earnestly desire to understand God's covenant with us as believers should carefully study John 14–17 and allow the Spirit of God to reveal His awesome promises and purposes through this beautiful passage.

A Covenant-Keeping God

"Therefore know that the LORD your God, He is God, the faithful God who keeps covenant and mercy for a thousand generations with those who love Him and keep His commandments" (Deuteronomy 7:9). God does not break His promises. Once He has entered into a covenant, His faithfulness is a sure thing. Consider God's tireless display of covenant keeping to David in the following quote from Bob Beckett's book *Commitment to Conquer*:

[God] honored David, for example, in the generations that followed that beloved king because David was a man after God's own heart. Here are two of the promises God gave David:

"When your days are fulfilled and you rest with your fathers, I will set up your seed after you, who will come from your body, and I will establish his kingdom. He shall build a house for My name, and I will establish the throne of his kingdom forever."

2 Samuel 7:12–13

Not long afterward, David's son Solomon disobeyed God by taking foreign women as wives and then worshiping their gods. God was angry and intended to tear Solomon's kingdom apart. But He said, "*Nevertheless I will not do it in your days, for the sake of your father David . . .*" (1 Kings 11:12). Two generations later we see David's grandson Abijam spared:

He walked in all the sins of his father, which he had done before him; his heart was not loyal to the LORD his God, as was the heart of his father David. Nevertheless for David's sake the LORD his God gave him a lamp in Jerusalem, by setting up his son after him and by establishing Jerusalem; because David did what was right in the eyes of the LORD, and had not turned aside from anything that He commanded him all the days of his life, except in the matter of Uriah the Hittite.

1 Kings 15:3–5

Then, 156 years after David's death, Judah was spared because David's great-grandchildren were living in the land: "The Lord would not destroy Judah, for the sake of his servant David, as He promised him to give a lamp to him and his sons forever" (2 Kings 8:19). Finally, a full 313 years later, Jerusalem was spared once again: "For I will defend this city, to save it for My own sake and for My servant David's sake" (2 Kings 19:34).[8]

To go one step further with this covenant, God promised to establish the throne of David's kingdom forever through his son Solomon. Jesus was, in fact, a descendant of David's through Solomon's line (see Matthew 1:6). David's throne, therefore, found its ultimate fulfillment in Jesus, who is called the Son of David, and of His Kingdom there shall be no end. God is a faithful, covenant-keeping God!

He Intends to Bless Us

The everlasting covenant is meant to bring all those who have come to a saving knowledge of Christ into their eternal destiny. This covenant provides tremendous promises that give us a hope for our eternal future. *But what about this life?*

The New Covenant promises to address issues for this life as well as eternity. God has a destiny for each of His children to fulfill in this lifetime. Therefore, He is longing to make covenant with every one of us in order to facilitate that destiny. Jeremiah 29:11–13 says,

> For I know the thoughts that I think toward you, says the LORD, thoughts of peace and not of evil, to give you a future and a hope. Then you will call upon Me and go and pray to

Me, and I will listen to you. And you will seek Me and find Me, when you search for Me with all your heart.

God yearns to give us a future and a hope. He has appropriated these things for every believer. But we, too, have a part to play in receiving them. In Jeremiah He says that when we call upon Him, He will listen, and when we search for Him with all our hearts, we will find Him. We must discover God's covenant plan for our personal lives. The only way to do that is to listen, search for Him with all our hearts and obey His commandments.

Covenant-Breaking Spirits

His purpose for making covenant is to bless us and move us into the destiny He has for us. The covenants He makes with us offer blessings of our inheritance, both here on earth and eternally. Covenants have tremendous spiritual implications. The purpose for making a covenant is to give a personal commitment, not only to the other party involved but also as a declaration to those outside the covenant. For example, in a marriage relationship, the wedding ring is a symbol of that covenant. Besides being a constant reminder to each party of the covenant agreement, it also says to the rest of the world that a marriage covenant is in place, so the wearer is not available to enter into other romantic or sexual relationships.

Likewise, when we enter into covenant relationship with God through the blood of Jesus Christ, demonic forces know that we are covered by His blood. We wear this as a spiritual, invisible covering. The blood of Jesus says to the enemy, "*Hands off!* This is not your territory!" Why, then, does the enemy seem to be able to steal away the inheritance of so many Christians? Why do countless Christians walk in defeat rather than victory, never reaching their full potential or destiny? It is because we have either not understood God's covenant plan or have chosen to live in disobedience to that covenant.

People with adultery in their hearts may find that a wedding ring actually makes someone else's spouse more attractive to them. They may pursue another's husband or wife with the intent of drawing that spouse into an adulterous affair. The spouse, at that point, must decide whether or not he or she will remain faithful to the marriage agreement. If the spouse does not remain faithful, he or she runs a risk of losing all the covenantal elements and rights of the marriage, and perhaps the marriage itself, because of his or her indiscretion.

In the spiritual realm, demonic forces are like the person trying to lure a spouse away from fidelity. The mission of the covenant-breaking spirit is to be an agent of Satan's quest to kill, steal and destroy. We must war to keep our covenants in place. Unless we come into full agreement with God's covenant plan for our lives, we are open targets, whether we know it or not, for these demonic forces to lure us into breaking away from our covenant with God. Once we have broken that covenant, we have stepped away from the blessings it provides.

Here is an example: A major part of our covenant with God is that we will have no other gods before Him (see Exodus 20:3). This is the first of the Ten Commandments, and God takes it very seriously. The commandment did not fall out of existence when Christ died for us; in fact, He reiterated the commandment by saying, "You shall love the LORD your God with all your heart, with all your soul, and with all your mind. This is the first and great commandment" (Matthew 22:37–38).

Demonic forces, however, are assigned to try to hook us into sin or idolatry. If we have sin in our lives that we are unwilling to give up or hold before the Lord with an open hand, saying, "Lord, do with this what You will," we ascribe to that thing a higher value than God. We have then broken this commandment and with it have compromised our covenant.

Whenever we compromise our covenant with God, we step away from the protection and blessings of that covenant. Without that protection, Satan is free to steal from us what God had intended to be part of our inheritance! We can kick and scream at the devil, telling him in Jesus' name to give us back sevenfold what we have lost. But until we repent before God and return to our place of right standing within His covenant, our protection against such thievery is gone. Satan can and does steal our inheritance and even our destiny when we have moved away from our covenant with God.

Covenant-breaking spirits can also cause us to break covenant with one another, which can cause reproach to come into our lives and even over the land we live on.

David learned this lesson the hard way. "Now there was a famine in the days of David for three years, year after year; and David inquired of the LORD. And the LORD answered, 'It is because of Saul and his bloodthirsty house, because he killed the Gibeonites'" (2 Samuel 21:1). What does this have to do with covenant breaking? The Gibeonites, whom Saul had killed, were another people who had entered into a covenant with Israel during Joshua's days to guarantee their safety. When Saul killed them, he broke that covenant agreement. As a result, a famine came upon the land and appropriate repentance had to occur in order to restore the land.

Covenant breaking is a serious matter with serious implications, especially when we consider that we and all that affects our lives can move out from under God's protection if we break covenant with Him.

In the final three chapters, I will show you the wars to come over covenant and religion, and what will become of us as we relate to the glorious eternal covenant.

8

The War over One New Man

Did you ever get disciplined as a child? "Spare the rod, then spoil the child!" was the prevailing philosophy in my parents' generation. For the most part, though, I was a very obedient child and had few altercations with those in authority above me. My mother had one rule: "Let me know where you are going and when you will be home in case I need to get in touch with you." Following this rule taught me how to stay within the time and space God has allotted me. I am sure this is one of the key disciplines that assisted in developing the Issachar anointing within me. The Bible says that without boundaries or vision a people perish (Proverbs 29:18). Learning to stay within God's boundaries has proved to be a saving grace as I have traveled the world to many nations.

When I was a child, I only violated this rule once, and it resulted in discipline. As a father I instilled its importance in my own children. Each time my children disregarded this boundary in their lives, they also encountered adverse circumstances. I hope I have enough strength to see my children's children operating in this paradigm.

Nations are God's children. "Ask of Me, and I will give You the nations for Your inheritance, and the ends of the earth for Your possession" (Psalm 2:8). He disciplines each nation to present to His Son. He created a model for the nations when He made covenant with Abraham. Israel is God's child—the firstborn nation of the world around which all other nations revolve and reconcile.

The Rod of God's Discipline

A true prophet must be aware of God's dealing with nations. God has a rod of authority that He uses when nations persist in obstinate disobedience. He does this until they submit themselves to obedience (see Revelation 2:27; Psalm 2:9). One of Holy Spirit's defining identities is Judge, and He convicts when error and injustice reigns. Any scriptural interpretation ignoring this understanding must be ruled an error and shunned. The Church that is filled and defined by the power of Holy Spirit will share with Him in ruling the nations with a rod of iron, as we see in Revelation 2:27. In this Scripture, we find God sealing and securing His saints who will reign with Him over the nations.

God always secures a place or portion of the heathen world from nation to nation in which His Church can be nurtured and mature. The place in the wilderness prepared of God (Revelation 12:6, 14)—the modern Babylon—will only be reserved until her time comes to be the greatest influence in the world. The world actually *hides* her, the Church, and provides an outward shelter for Her development. She is very much like Moses in Pharaoh's court. Though the Church is in the world, she must not look like the world. Therefore, while she is being nourished and provided for, she must always keep an acute awareness of her true identity and whom she is there to represent. She is like Daniel in Babylon, leading like Joseph led in Egypt. This is the Esther Church of the future!

In Revelation 12 we find the Church seeking, from apostolic age to apostolic age, a place of refuge. In the midst of her seeking, she is developing a testimony of overcoming: *the word of her testimony.* She becomes selfless and devoted to the heavenly will of the Father, even if this means that she loves not her life until death. Suddenly, in the midst of conflict, the blood of the Lamb in her begins to arise and she triumphs.

The danger comes when the Church is tempted by Babylon, begins to embrace its ways and then commits fornication with the world. Instead of overcoming, she is overcome by the world. We then become common, and our defining, sharpening edge is dulled. We no longer transform society but are conformed to look like the blueprint of the enemy.

Overthrow the Ancestral Altar

Once I heard my dear friend Dutch Sheets share that he felt the ruling spirit in America was Baal, the demonic ruler of Canaan. Overthrowing the altar of Baal in Gideon's day (Judges 6) meant dethroning the ruler of his father's household and the people. Gideon then led the people to realign with the God of their father, Abraham, and move back into a place of restoration. For us, this means that to change a nation, the arising generation must have a counterrevolution fueled by the Spirit of God.

The account of Gideon illustrates the connection between family and the coming war. Gideon was representing
his family, and that led him to represent a nation. Before he
responded to God's visitation, he represented the aligned
structures of religion and mammon. To overthrow a structure, however, requires a visitation from heaven. We can
see why this visitation for Gideon had to be drastically
revolutionary—He had to overthrow his father's altar to
Baal!

When we consider the significance of family that I presented in chapter 7, we see why this was a major shift in
thought processes of that time. The iniquities of the father
must be overturned for the next generation to advance. If
we go to war without recognizing our fathers' iniquities, we
will be weakened in the heat of battle.

Sometimes our continued warfare makes us willing to
change course. Gideon was tired of threshing wheat in a
winepress. Like many of the people of Israel, he was tired
of the harvest being stolen each year by the Midianites, yet
fear seemed to rule. Many times a robbing spirit overtakes
us at our time of harvest, but because we are fearful, we do
not stop to call on a God that can change things around us.
Gideon was not a confident soldier, but once he was willing
to go to war, God manifested Himself as Jehovah Shalom.
Shalom means "peace" or "wholeness." Many times peace
will not come until we go to war.

Even in Gideon's day, the people dissented over who would
war and who would not. When this happens in a nation,
God must use His rod to discipline the Church and create
a separation and remnant for the future. Gideon ended up
going to battle with three hundred. This is an example of
the triumphant reserve!

Covenant Conflicts in the Earth

We look at judgment from one perspective, but God views judgment as the beginning of restoration. I awakened recently with the Spirit of God saying, *I do not see things the same way you see things. Therefore, gain My perspective.* We must see the way He sees if we are to survive and thrive.

The Gentiles are in a time of threshing, separating the wheat from the tares. He will continue to discipline His people from nation to nation until the fullness of the Gentiles occurs. While this is happening to the Church, He is preserving the Jews. Eventually, the two will become one new man, but not without warfare. In this warfare we are seeing the following:

1. *Aliyah*—the Jews are and will continue returning to Israel.
2. Jesus as *Yeshua* is becoming a reality to many Jews.
3. An awareness of latter-day scenarios are being awakened in mankind as prophecies are being fulfilled.
4. Jerusalem is becoming *the* focal point of the earth.
5. The enemy against Israel is intensifying his efforts. Arab countries continue to create confusion over the two-state system in Palestine when, in reality, they are the ones rejecting the conditions of peace. This gives Satan the upper hand in his attempt to orchestrate Israel's destruction. The accuser runs rampant in the nations and misrepresents Israel.
6. Nations are aligning together against Israel. In the next ten years, we will see an acceleration of this dynamic (see Zechariah 12:2–3).
7. A new spiritual revival and restoration is occurring in the Church. How nations receive this awakening will

result in their accelerated transformations. The Church is rising in the midst of society and having Her voice heard.

8. A new personal, spiritual baptism is bubbling in God's people. This is causing each one to learn to rejoice and enjoy life in the midst of warfare.

9. China is becoming more and more predominant in her rule, influence and ownership in the world. The decade from September 2016 through September 2026 will be the season of transformation of the Church in China. There will be great conflicts between the civil government of the state and the Kingdom government of God! The remnant in China will arise and advance. Because of their focus on Israel, there will be a great move of God. The Chinese government will attempt to do what Constantine did in legalizing the Church, but the Church will prevail.

10. Russia will become increasingly jealous and aggressive to gain control of the world. Many disgruntled nations will shift their allegiance to Russia, fully embrace her philosophy and submit to her rule.

11. The war of wealth will intensify and become a cyber-mammon conflict to wear down the saints and keep them from seeing a manifestation of God's glory.

12. The saints will rebel against the enemy, understand the antichrist system and develop new storehouses, as in the days of Joseph.

13. Religious wars will escalate in Islamic antichrist terrorist structures and in Babylonian Christian structures, which go by the name of Christ and have a form of godliness but deny His power, instituting the world's methods in their operations.

14. A new wave of martyrdom will occur, and the world will see the difference between religious zeal and love for the one true God.

The result of these factors is a tremendous separation in both Jew and Gentile worlds. This separation, both physical and spiritual, produces a reformed one new man. The dynamic of Jew and Gentile walking together, experiencing the Spirit of God, will be evident by 2026. The sealed remnant will be preserved from the Antichrist. This is the triumphant reserve that rules and influences on behalf of God in the nations and is preserved "from the presence of the serpent" (Revelation 12:14).

The Accusing Adversary Loses Strength in the End

When Christ appeared before God as our Advocate, Satan, the accusing adversary, could no longer appear against us! He was cast out *judicially* (see Romans 8:33–34), and we began to gain wisdom to enforce his dethroning. As the triumphant ones, we can go to the Father, having been given access by the Son, and receive the wisdom necessary to dethrone the enemy within our spheres of authority in the areas he attempts to rule and reign. We are positioned, in the midst of our social structures and cultures, to rule in the days ahead.

A great war is coming between God's army—those of us who know God—and the forces that wish to represent the antichrist rule of injustice. *But God!* We are not alone! The host of heaven, angelic forces sent by the Lord to assist in earth's warfare, begin to encamp around us. The one new man rises and makes peace through the blood of His cross. By Him, all deviations from the will of heaven are reconciled.

All things are aligned unto Himself—"whether things on earth or things in heaven" (Colossians 1:20).

Therefore, we must not despise the discipline that is occurring in our lives, our ministries, our businesses and our nations. This discipline is separating us to become a powerful people that represent the returning Lord Jesus Christ as our Head and Cornerstone in the coming days. We must watch as God's promise unfolds in the earth. We must watch as Israel becomes the first nation and rises and prepares to host the King. We must watch as nations receive and respond to discipline from the rod of the Lord. How they respond reveals their true character as sheep or goat nations.

He Is Faithful to His Promise

God promised Abraham land, wealth, children and a heritage of multiplication. The promise was not bound to one group in time but extended from Abraham to David to the prophets to God's triumphant Bride, who is arising. We must trust His promises today with a healthy resonance of "Yes and amen!" Failure to hold fast and not trust in God's promise is our danger (see Psalm 106:24; Numbers 14:1–35).

Think of Israel. They were brought out of Egypt miraculously. They began their journey toward God's best but stopped short of faith becoming reality. They actually entered, touched and tasted God's best for them but chose to not occupy what had been given. They did not have the strength needed to overtake what was holding captive their destiny. Instead, they turned back and chose a wilderness form of life and worship. The leaders of that generation actually spoke against what had been given, and their unbelief ruled and spread like a virus. They died without ever experiencing all that Father longed to give them. From generation to generation, many have followed this pattern instead of arising, warring and possessing the inheritance that has been promised by a faithful God.

Promise means to announce beforehand something that will become reality at a later date (see Romans 1:2; 2 Corinthians 9:5). Once something is announced, we must await its day of unveiling. The promises of God are "Yes and amen." We must verbally align ourselves with what has been said and announced. How we repeat and respond to the announcement of God's will determines our future.

Along the journey toward fulfillment of the promise, we may make bad decisions and choices that seem unfaithful or disloyal. These choices, though they hinder the time of manifestation, do not stop the God of the promise from maintaining His faithfulness concerning what He has announced. He makes and keeps promises in spite of the failure and disobedience of His people. If we keep seeking, however, we will find!

Within the promise of God is our providential care, and because of the promise of God, we have ultimate victory over the devil. We can look to Abraham as our covenant example. All he had to do to receive the promise was begin his journey out of bondage and move toward the land of benefits. He had to respond to God. He made mistakes, but overall his heart kept moving forward. The same holds true for us!

Keep Moving into the New

The Lord, who initiated the first covenant with man, also promised and provided a New Covenant in spite of man's shortcomings (see Jeremiah 31:31–34). God writes His Word

199

on the hearts of His people. That Word cannot be erased or removed. The Word can grow dim, but we have an Advocate who is always working on our behalf to cause the Word to shine. The Third Person of the Godhead, the promised Spirit, keeps manifesting to convict and discipline those who represent the will of heaven on earth for their unrighteous actions (see Romans 8:9–13). A true servant trusts in the promise of God. Of our Messiah, Jesus of Nazareth, the fulfillment of the promise of a Savior from the seed of David (Acts 13:23, 32; 26:6; Romans 1:2; 4:13; 9:4), it was recorded, "He trusts in God" (Matthew 27:43 NIV).

All of God's promises have eternal and spiritual significance (Hebrews 4:1; 6:17; 11:9). Father sent the Son to reveal the perfection of the promise. Only through our alignment with the Son can the manifold, or multicolored and many faceted, blessings manifest. Only through Him can our hope exist. Here are a few of those manifestations:

- Life and eternal life
- The Kingdom in us advancing (James 2:5)
- Christ's "coming" and joining us to lead in an ultimate triumph (Revelation 5)
- New heavens and a new earth coming down (2 Peter 3:13) and being seen
- The promise of the Spirit, described by Jesus as "the Promise of My Father" (Luke 24:49; Acts 1:4), which was first fulfilled at Pentecost
- The demonstration of power, as seen in the book of Acts
- The ultimate triumph over the enemy who has opposed, hindered, postponed and attempted to remove the record of the manifestation of the promise.

We must diligently pursue and watch for these promises in our time. God promised me when I was eighteen that He would "restore what I had lost." Over the years I trusted. I chose to believe and obey every condition that He placed in my path for this manifestation to occur. I have watched after that word my entire adult life, and I have seen measures of its manifestation.

From Giant to Dragon

As we discussed in the last chapter, much of our warfare is linked to the testing of our faith. Eventually, however, the war shifts from us to a greater field that needs to be conquered. As Israel's most famous king, David always relied on the testimony of his last victory in the battle of his present war. When Israel faced Goliath, a giant representing the enemy nation of the Philistines, he recited the record of what he had accomplished to convince Saul that he could fight in the intensifying conflict:

> Your servant kept his father's sheep. And when there came a lion or again a bear and took a lamb out of the flock, I went out after it and smote it and delivered the lamb out of its mouth; and when it arose against me, I caught it by its beard and smote it and killed it. Your servant killed both the lion and the bear; and this uncircumcised Philistine shall be like one of them, for he has defied the armies of the living God!
>
> 1 Samuel 17:34–36 AMPC

David knew that what he could testify to in the past could be used as the springboard for the future. Look back at your times of triumph. Rehearse your victories. Speak your testimony. In the midst of your next conflict, your testimony will be a weapon to overcome whatever is your past. David called upon the name of the Lord; we must learn to do the same! The name of the Lord was stamped and displayed in his testimony. That is the name that overcomes what is in your path.

Great wars are coming, and giants in our lives and on our paths must be addressed. Representing us is an Advocate who overcame. Along with our access to Him, we have the angelic hosts at His command. I believe we are presently facing the giants that are attempting to stop the cause of our King, some of which I have discussed in earlier chapters. In the days ahead, however, we will move from giants to contend with the dragon and his dark angelic forces!

We must understand the rebellion that arose from unfaithful angels and their leader. Yes, there has been an ultimate victory and judgment against this foe through the action of the Messiah, but now the enforcement of that judgment intensifies. We, like David, must stand for the cause of the Kingdom and against hindering opponents. We can only overcome and triumph by aligning with the faithful angels and their archangel, Michael, when dispatched from heaven. The beast, false prophet and their hordes are being readied for confrontation. The Son of Man, His hosts of angel armies and His armies of human saints are aligning for a victorious display of glory in the earth (Revelation 19:14–21).

We, the triumphant ones, will become victorious in our thinking and actions! The conflict on earth is reflected in the conflict of angels in heaven. In Daniel 10, for example, we find Daniel contending for revelation on earth, while Michael, the prince or presiding angel of the Jewish nation, contended in heaven so that the revelation could come. As I have stated, the conflict in heaven has already been decided judicially against

Satan, the dragon; from the time of Christ's resurrection and ascension the decision was made. But this decision receives its actual completion in the execution of judgment by the angels who were there to cast Satan out of heaven.

Because of our Lord's ascension, the dragon has no judicial standing against the believing elect. Luke 10:18 (KJV) states, "I beheld Satan as lightning fall from heaven." As Michael fought with Satan about the body of Moses, the mediator of the Old Covenant (Jude 9), so now the mediator of the New Covenant, by offering His sinless body in sacrifice, arms Michael with power to renew and finish the conflict by a complete victory. Not only is he empowered to win, he has an aligned army in earth ready to join him. This is the triumphant reserve!

Our Advocate against the Accuser

Through Israel's unbelief, Satan has held ground against the elect nation, appearing before God as accuser. When Messiah seated Himself next to Father and then seated us with Him, the accuser's ultimate defeat was inevitable. Just the matter of perfect timing separates the manifestation of this defeat.

We are at the eve of a great restoration. Satan, a defeated foe, has continued to stand and attempt to hold his ground in heaven against Israel. He has withstood and attempted to accuse the saints and any others who have stood with Israel. He has hated anyone who has aligned with God's covenant. In the end, however, the adversary and all who have aligned with him will be removed.

One of my favorite verses is from the account of the prophet Zechariah: "The LORD rebuke you, Satan! The LORD who has chosen Jerusalem rebuke you!" (Zechariah 3:2). The people of God had sinned, leading them into a seventy-year captivity. Captivity of a child or people of God has a time limit; eventually the time comes when one's discipline and warfare ends. Now was the time for this same people to finish restoring the Temple of His glory. Satan longed to remind them of their past sins. This condemnation was meant to slow their progress and hinder their ability in the future.

Joshua, the high priest, as representative of God's nation, had to be reclothed for the event ahead. Satan uses our past in an attempt to stop our future. But God, who is not in time, knows our past and in a moment can absolve us from our wrongdoing. Once His discipline has been completed in our lives, He loves to see us advance. We are still representing God's purposes in the earth, and Satan, as adversary, is determined to stand against God's right hand of strength. He still contends against God's assignments that lead us into a victorious future.

Satan is constantly resisting Israel's justification based on her past. He does the same with you. *But God!* There comes a time when the adversary of mankind is confronted and rebuked by the King of kings. When the Lord is ready for us to move forward and complete His purposes, nothing can stop that progression. He removes the iniquitous identity of our past and clothes us for our victorious future. Do you not love this?

There will come a time when all the heavens will be cleansed. In Revelation 12:7–9 we find Michael, the prince angel, casting the great dragon out from the third heaven. Michael will lead a troop to ultimately overtake Satan in the first heaven, earth's realm. All things will be reconciled unto Christ in heaven (Colossians 1:20), and there shall be peace in heaven (Luke 19:38). Though the *judicial* sentence to that effect received its ratification at Christ's ascension, "spiritual wickedness in high places" still attempts to rule. Satan, the dragon, will be *actually* and *finally* cast out of all heavens. This cannot be fully accomplished without the aligned, faith-filled saints being jointly fit together (Ephesians 4). There is a climax of this war, and we win! Then no place will be found for the dragon.

Bob McGregor, a bowling Hall of Famer and a good friend, recently sent me the following exhortation:

> *When the angels of heaven are arrayed for battle, they wait only for My word that releases them to engage the enemy. The Body of Christ should respond in the same way—not in obedience to man, or even to many men. They should only respond if and when their heavenly Commander in Chief has first spoken. This does not mean that all will go to war at the same time and have the same tasks or targets, for surely your varied gifts and callings fit into different parts of My battle plan. But, to wage war effectively, there must be unity within the Body and its leadership. Prepare yourself and stay properly aligned with the chain of command I have set over you. This is a time when I am drawing together members from My worldwide Church. You may not all think alike, but all report ultimately to Me through the leadership I have put in place. Do not allow your preconceived ideas and traditions to become stumbling blocks. There is one Body, and I am bringing it together to stand undivided against the enemy. Stay in formation and know that the Lord of Armies has left nothing to chance.*[1]

The Ultimate Triumph of Blood and Testimony

Satan has fallen, but now a greater manifestation of that fall is seen. His role as man's accuser is fully revenged by the Lord. The Old Testament dispensation could not overcome him, but the fullness of the New Covenant does. Seated positionally, man now shuts down all access by Satan and his demons and enforces the power of the resurrected Christ in the earth. Satan loses his power against Israel. His rage on earth is greater toward the end, for "he knows that he has a short time" (Revelation 12:12). Israel can look forward to these promises: "And her Child [Israel] was caught up to God and His throne" (Revelation 12:5) and "The kingdoms of this world have become the kingdoms of our Lord and of His Christ" (Revelation 11:15). Israel resumes her place.

Because Jesus' blood was shed, Satan's accusations have been made unanswerable. The blood of the Lamb has met every charge that will ever come against one of God's elect. The Lord's obedience will be fulfilled.

On account of the word of their faithful testimony, even unto death, the triumphant one new man is sealed as victor. By virtue of the blood of the Lamb, our testimony trumps every accusation. We are a people who have passed over! We confess to the world and the enemy that we are worshipers of the slain Lamb. Through this confession, we will have ultimate victory over the beast! We embrace the love of the Father who gave His Son for our redemption. Because of His death and triumphant overcoming power in us, we triumph. He overcame death and hell; therefore we overcome death and hell. We do not love our lives to death because our eyes have been opened to see into a realm of eternity. Satan no longer has a right to tabernacle with man. The tabernacle of man is now the tabernacle of God.

9

The War of Religion

I think you can surmise that the war ahead revolves around religion. Poverty and infirmity align with religion to wear down God's people, but in the end we triumph. The Antichrist has a final goal: to take over the way the saints worship. No pulpit is without conflict in days ahead. The influencing force on the saints is mammon, which moves on religious systems in an attempt to gain control of lives, properties and all types of freedom. Mammon must not hold God's people captive to a poverty mentality. This does not include just being poor—poverty has a voice that causes us to think in our minds that God is not able.

In the days of Ahab and Jezebel, there was a great religious war between Elijah (representing a Holy God) and the prophets of Baal (representing Jezebel). Naboth and his vineyard were caught in the midst of the changes in control of government systems. Ahab was not strong enough to take

Naboth's land, so Jezebel devised an accusation to illegally remove him and present the coveted booty to Ahab. Both Jezebel
and Ahab were judged accordingly. This account in 1 Kings
21 is the precursor of what is to come. There is a great war
over your portion. The enemy wants your field, the portion
that God has allotted you. This is your inheritance. We must
proclaim, as Naboth did, "The LORD forbid that I should give
the inheritance of my fathers to you!" (1 Kings 21:3).

Religious wars are often the root of conflicts. Religion
empowered by covetousness is the cause of warfare in the
earth. Pride promotes strife:

> Where do wars and fights come from among you? Do they
> not come from your desires for pleasure that war in your
> members? You lust and do not have. You murder and covet
> and cannot obtain. You fight and war. Yet you do not have
> because you do not ask. You ask and do not receive, because
> you ask amiss, that you may spend it on your pleasures.
> Adulterers and adulteresses! Do you not know that friend-
> ship with the world is enmity with God? Whoever therefore
> wants to be a friend of the world makes himself an enemy of
> God. Or do you think that the Scripture says in vain, "The
> Spirit who dwells in us yearns jealously"?
>
> James 4:1–5

This goes back to Cain and Abel. Their war over worship
and giving created the formation of iniquitous roots in the
structures, cultures and foundational building of the societies
of mankind. One of the major iniquitous forces in Christian
lives especially is *God robbing*. I believe God robbing aligns
with religion and infirmity to form a strong three-fold cord
that is difficult to break. To be triumphant, we must learn
to detangle and overcome this cord in our lives.

We must *give* our way into the future. The main reason why most people find it hard to give is because they are bound by the last strand of the three-fold cord: the spirit of religion. In Matthew 16:6, Jesus warns us to beware of the Pharisees, who were religious—they even tithed—but either did not know God or were unwilling to change when God was ready to do something new. The spirit of religion resists change. I believe that it is one of the strongest spirits to break.

The Main Operations of Religious Spirits

Religious spirits are demonically empowered philosophies that narrow our expression of the God of heaven and prevent Him from displaying free, expressive worship in earth. The religious spirit is a deceptive force that labors through the ages to stop the progress of the Church. Religion empowers tradition by adding fixed rules that originate in man and is itself empowered by *methodai* spirits—linked with methods of administration—to hold us captive to one way of expressing a multifaceted God. Whereas order sets events in place to give you great authority, religious spirits use methods to capture you in a Greek way of thought that blinds you from divine inspiration and order.

Religion is not a bad thing when we adhere to the word's literal meaning: *to consider divine things*. The word *religion* has three meanings in the Word of God:

- Outward religious acts, such as praying and going to church
- The feeling of absolute dependence
- The observance of moral law as a divine institution

209

James 1:26–27 defines religion from the Christian point of view:

> If anyone among you thinks he is religious, and does not bridle his tongue but deceives his own heart, this one's religion is useless. Pure and undefiled religion before God and the Father is this: to visit orphans and widows in their trouble, and to keep oneself unspotted from the world.

Religion is linked with worship. When pure, it is very powerful. Religion can also be defined, however, as an organized system of doctrine with an approved pattern of behavior. Behavior has to demonstrate a proper form of worship. This is where we move from pure and undefiled religion to ritual. Demons of doctrine rob individuals of their freedom to worship a Holy God in purity by instituting rules and regulations for their worship.

I have always been a creative thinker and an expressive worshiper. In addition, I have been known throughout the Body of Christ as a modern-day prophet who expresses the heart and mind of God. Because of this, I have always had to maneuver past spirits of religion that resist this gift of God. Demons hate that revelation from God can be expressed in the earth. They do not mind us believing in a historical account of God. When we appropriate the power of God in our lives today, however, demonic forces are called to attention. They must stop God's Kingdom from expressing life in the earth. They resist those gifts in the Body that bring revelatory freedom to its members. They attempt to stone the revelation of apostles and prophets, because this revealed word establishes God's foundation in the Church for this age. Religious spirits attempt to defy God's order of governmental gifts in the Church for victory in the world, as we read in 1 Corinthians 12:28: "First apostles, second prophets."

Religious spirits can also deny change! Our processes of thought aid the Spirit of God to produce change in the earth, but the carnal mind is in enmity with God. Religious spirits attempt to block strategic thinking. They can make individuals become so routinized, or in a rut, that they do not want to shift into today's methods for victory. These spirits hold us captive to old methods of the last season.

In the New Testament, the Lord's disciples had to have revelation of who He was, who they were and who their enemy was. The Pharisees had a choice either to deny the divine nature of God's Son or to align themselves with Him. They had to choose either to keep rules in place that prevented behavioral change in worship or to begin to worship in Spirit and truth. Most failed in making the choice that could have changed their lives, their families and their society.

Therefore, in Matthew 16:18–19, we find Jesus taking the keys of the Kingdom of heaven from the scribes and Pharisees and giving them to the future leaders who would defy religion and lead the Church into its future. The same holds true today. We must know who Christ is, who we are and who our enemy is, and we must choose to follow the Spirit as He leads us into days of transformation. Romans 12:2 reads, "Do not be conformed to this world, but be transformed by the renewing of your mind, that you may prove what is that good and acceptable and perfect will of God." The word *transform* means to change, transfigure or experience a metamorphosis, such as a caterpillar that is transformed into a butterfly. The Lord told His people Israel that they could change from being worms to being new, sharp instruments with teeth that would thresh the mountains (see Isaiah 41:14–16).

The Lord says,

> *Fear not! Do not fear embracing the paradigms that will pro-
> duce change. Do not fear confronting the enemy. Do not fear
> the next great move of the Spirit of God. Do not fear letting
> go of worship methods in the Church that have caused you
> to become comfortable. Defy the spirits of religion around
> you and move with boldness into your future!*

Watchers of the Covenant

We must watch past religion to make sure the true power of
God is displayed in the earth. Religion has a form, but glory
and relationship with a true God has a demonstration. We
must watch the vineyard God has given us. We must also
watch day and night until Jerusalem becomes a praise in
the earth. Elijah knew when the time of rain was to come,
and he pulled the rain from a heavenly realm into the earth
realm. He had prophesied that there would be no rain for
three and a half years, and he had to watch after that word
until the time of manifestation came. We must do the same.

Having your kids live in Israel keeps you on your toes
in warfare praying. Amber, my daughter-in-law, shared the
following as she and her family endured the war in Israel:

> As we enter our sixth year living in Israel, it is clear we have
> learned a great deal. To watch over God's covenant with
> many in the land of Israel is a tremendous call. During the
> last war, I constantly saw the words *watchers of the cov-
> enant*. I realized that this call was being extended to our
> generation, yet I saw a struggle for several of us to commit
> to and endure the tests necessary to see Israel remain at the
> forefront of the Church's desire. To love Israel sounds easier
> than it is in reality. Because we grow up with Bible stories,

we romanticize the lives we read about. Though this is not always a bad thing, the manifestation is a progression. It is not a month-long call, or a year of pressing, but a call to forever.

When I visualize this, I always see the Temple Mount, no matter where I am or what I am doing. The reason this is important is because God used Israel to display Himself to us. If He is the God of yesterday, today and tomorrow, and if He never changes His mind about Israel, then He will never change His mind about us. The way that God has kept covenant with Israel assures me that He will be constant in my personal life as well. If we watch with Him over His land and people, we are really watching over ourselves, our families and our future.

This war is over whose voice will be heard from Zion, but it is also over whose voice will be heard in our personal lives. Saying yes to this call means blood, sweat, tears and sorrows. Our hope is in the Messiah, Jesus Christ of Nazareth, who came and will come again. Because of this we can find joy, as we are anchored in Him. A dear friend, Anne Tate, said that a season of watching produces "the best of times and the worst of times! You identify, travail and labor, but you end up *seeing* the hand of God manifest in your life."

Most often when God brings us through something hard, it marks us in a special way that is hard to forget. God recently showed me how important it is to take an account or make a record of our testimonies. We overcome by the blood of the Lamb and the word of our testimony. Since the devil seeks to kill, steal and destroy, we must keep remembrance of our testimonies.

What has God brought you through? You need to remember it so that in every challenge and battle, you use your last testimony of what God did for you. Israel has many testimonies as a nation. My husband, Daniel, and I have friends who have fought in some of the major wars of the country, and they know the goodness of God over the nation.

Israel can be perplexing. When in warfare, we can lose sight of why we are fighting and even how we got to our present place. A friend once confided that she was not sure why she got married or chose to live in Israel. I told her that the enemy was trying to steal her testimony so that he could steal her future. I also quoted my father-in-law, saying that God is not bound by time and that He can go back in time so that her testimony could be restored to her family. Not knowing our testimony or keeping a record of what God has done for us opens the door to the enemy and puts our vision at risk of being skewed or even destroyed. Through living in times of physical war, we have learned that testimony is key to victory. This applies to every aspect of our lives. You must keep a record of your testimony so that you triumph over the enemy.

The Joy of the Lord Triumphs

Those great insights come from one who lives in the greatest covenant war fields on earth. The most important thing to remember in war is that we must keep some sort of joy to maintain the ability and strength to fight. Life should be filled with joy, for "the joy of the LORD is your strength" (Nehemiah 8:10).[1]

My son Daniel, Amber's husband, confirms the importance of preserving joy. An adventurer at heart, he shared his own interesting insights about life in Israel.

If there is one thing we have learned living in Israel, it is that we need the joy of the Lord to sustain us in times of warfare. Whatever form war takes—whether spiritual attack or physical combat—the joy that only God can bring becomes our strength. Living in a nation constantly at war, we have learned that physical warfare is a direct result of spiritual

214

conflict spilling over into the earth. This might sound like overspiritualization, but I have seen it happen on many occasions. Those who have experienced physical combat know that a sense of chaos accompanies warfare. It is difficult to describe to someone who has never been in this situation. Even soldiers and policemen, if they have never experienced it, often lack a full understanding of the physical and emotional toll that warfare can take.

As we walk out our lives with the Lord, we will experience times of warfare on a spiritual level that will test our strength. You will find that spiritual warfare can have many of the same effects as physical combat if you allow trauma to take hold. As I sought the Lord over the concept of warfare, He began to show me how joy is the key to overcoming trauma and maintaining the vision that He has over our lives.

In John 15, Jesus speaks to His disciples concerning the relationship He desires and how we are to remain in Him while He remains in us. In verse 11, He goes on to say, "I have told you this so that my joy may be in you and that your joy may be complete" (NIV). When I read this passage, the Lord quickened me in a new way to the fact that it is and always has been His desire that we should live lives full of joy. Then He reminded me that joy is one of the fruits of the Spirit: "But the fruit of the Spirit is love, joy, peace, patience, kindness, goodness, faithfulness, gentleness, self-control; against such things there is no law" (Galatians 5:22–23 NASB). When we begin to understand that God is the one who fills us with joy, our desire will be to remain in Him and for Him to remain in us.

Joy strengthens us and allows us to not only endure hardship but also gain strength and maturity from our struggles.

In the book of James, the twelve tribes are instructed to take joy even in their trials and to look at hardship as an opportunity: "Consider it pure joy, my brothers and sisters, whenever you face trials of many kinds, because you know that the testing of your faith produces perseverance. Let perseverance finish its work so that you may be mature and complete, not lacking anything" (James 1:1–4 NIV).

Just as a soldier on the battlefield gains understanding from his first experience in combat, a strengthening comes through testing that produces perseverance. On a personal level we will all experience the draining effect of spiritual warfare. We live in a world full of enemies who will persecute anyone who submits his or her life to God's will. In Proverbs 10 we see a relationship between hope and joy: "The hope of righteous people leads to joy, but the eager waiting of wicked people comes to nothing" (Proverbs 10:28 GW). When we place our hope in Jesus, He fills us with His joy.

As I began to consider the role of righteousness in producing joy, God reminded me of some of my favorite verses in the Bible. "Blessed are those who hunger and thirst for righteousness, for they will be filled. . . . Blessed are the pure in heart, for they will see God" (Matthew 5:6, 8 NIV). When we hunger and thirst for righteousness, we come with expectation that we will be filled. When God fills us with His Holy Spirit, the fruits of the Spirit will become manifest in our lives. When joy takes hold, it changes our understanding of our circumstances, and the hope we have in Jesus becomes the focus of our future.

> I consider that our present sufferings are not worth comparing with the glory that will be revealed in us. The creation waits in eager expectation for the sons of God to be revealed. For the creation was subjected to frustration, not by its own

choice, but by the will of the one who subjected it, in hope
that the creation itself will be liberated from its bondage to
decay and brought into the glorious freedom of the children
of God.

Romans 8:18–21 NIV1984

Romans 8 speaks of this world's bondage to decay and
the glorious freedom that is the hope of liberation that we
have in Jesus. If trauma is allowed to take root in us, decay
and frustrations of this world will be the result. This passage
also reminds us that our present sufferings are not worth
comparing with the glory that will be revealed in us.

When soldiers are trained in the military, a great amount
of time and effort is dedicated to learning how to disassoci-
ate physical discomfort from the ability to function on the
battlefield. This process, which is taught in basic training, is
necessary for a soldier to focus on victory even in the midst
of extremely traumatic and often chaotic situations. If you
speak to soldiers or police officers who have experienced
this firsthand, most will tell you that the fear passes and the
training kicks in, allowing you to act decisively in the moment. After the fight comes a time to address trauma and
assess victories.

When the enemy attacks us on a spiritual level and our
situation begins to look hopeless, we must remember the
Lord's will for those who follow Him.

"For I know the plans I have for you," declares the LORD,
"plans to prosper you and not to harm you, plans to give you
hope and a future. Then you will call on me and come and
pray to me, and I will listen to you. You will seek me and
find me when you seek me with all your heart."

Jeremiah 29:11–13 NIV

Daniel continued to share:

Through my experience in law enforcement, I noticed that there is something different about those who reach command positions. A good leader will have a different presence than your average soldier, characterized by a sense of peace and confidence in situations that would cause trauma in most. This demeanor is gained from years of experience in warfare and the knowledge that victory is attainable. King David was a mighty warrior that dedicated his life to worship and wrote much about how the joy of the Lord sustained him. "You will show me the path of life; in Your presence is fullness of joy; at Your right hand are pleasures forevermore" (Psalm 16:11 NKJV). We need to remain in God's presence to experience the fullness of His joy. When we come before the Lord in worship, He restores our vision and shows us the path of life. When we go forth rejoicing, He will meet us in our circumstances.

In Jeremiah's letter to the Jewish exiles in Babylon, the will of God becomes manifest in Jeremiah's words as he speaks to the Jewish people at one of the hardest points in their history. God's will is to give you a hope and a future! If we hold on to that in times of trouble, then we will not lose sight of our victory. God sets us at peace even in the hardest circumstances this life can bring.

"Rejoice in the Lord always. I will say it again: Rejoice! Let your gentleness be evident to all. The Lord is near. Do not be anxious about anything, but in every situation, by prayer and petition, with thanksgiving, present your requests to God. And the peace of God, which transcends all understanding, will guard your hearts and your minds in Christ Jesus" (Philippians 4:4–7 NIV).

Isaiah also spoke about this joy in Isaiah 55 and how we can have confidence that not a word the Lord has spoken will be voided:

So is my word that goes out from my mouth: It will not return to me empty, but will accomplish what I desire and achieve the purpose for which I sent it. You will go out in joy and be led forth in peace; the mountains and hills will burst into song before you, and all the trees of the field will clap their hands.

Isaiah 55:11–12 NIV

God has a peace that transcends all understanding. When we rejoice before the Lord and give our battles to Him, our hearts and minds will be guarded in Christ Jesus. His peace covers trauma and allows God to fill us with joy.

As we walk through life, God will carry us from victory to victory, and this will strengthen our testimony. Allow God to fill you with joy today and take hold of the words He has spoken over your life. Understand that God's word will not return void, and allow Him to strengthen you in your battles. Remember that victory is attainable and there is a peace that passes understanding. Let the trials of this life become your testimony, and take joy in the fact that trials produce perseverance. Remember that God's will for you is a hope and a future!

A Three-Fold Cord That Will Remake the Earth

A three-fold cord cannot easily be broken. In the coming days, wealth will be shaken and economies will change, and much of this will be rooted in a three-fold cord that will intensify warfare and constrict us, as if lassoed, so as to capture our life flow. This will produce a poverty mentality. As we move into this season, we must start addressing those forces that have been sent by Satan to hinder us from seeing our destiny manifest.

Religion is one factor in this three-fold cord. Our restoration cannot be released while God is tightly locked in a box. Satan is a liar and a thief, and his religion looses condemnation and causes us to be judgmental. Therefore, the Lord must shake us loose from religion. His Spirit shakes loose lies and old judgments that formed in the past. Isaiah 58 says that if you will pray and fast, letting God determine the fast for you (do not do it religiously), and if you will put away the pointing of that finger and looking outward, He will begin to break forth your light, and your healing will spring up. Let Him shake loose your healing.

Another factor in the three-fold cord is mammon. As I said earlier, much shaking occurs in shifting, trendsetting times. The prophet Haggai prophesied that God would shake us until all our old mindsets had been shaken off, until such a time that "the latter glory of this house will be greater than the former" (Haggai 2:9 NASB). The Lord says that He will shake the wealth of nations and gold and silver will become His (see verses 7–8). When He shakes loose wealth, we must become the conduits for that wealth to flow so we can build His prototype necessary to reflect His Kingdom in the earth from season to season.

Among the things He shakes loose are new levels of communion, vision and relationship with Himself; our identities for the future; and the ability to complete the projects we have begun. The Lord showed me in January 1986, for instance, that by the end of January 1996, the government of God would have begun to change. Then He showed me that by the end of 2006, His government would be in a new mature state. He showed me that in 2016, His Kingdom government would have been freed to create shaking in the earth. By 2026, we are to be a mighty Kingdom influencing earth in a great rearranging and realigning of nations.

Though we must not trust in riches, we must have supply to advance. Many invest in the stock market in hope of increasing their assets and developing a nest egg for their future. We love to see the market climb and produce increase. That makes the stock market prone to control one's future.

In reality stocks and the market can be easily manipulated. Economies like that of the United States seem strong so long as the stock market in that country appears strong. Fake, manipulative financial bubbles, however, can paint a wrong picture of the resource structure of a nation. The danger in trusting in a bubble is that it easily bursts. We must watch carefully in the future concerning financial supply lines:

- The drilling of natural assets will shift greatly. The oil-driven economies of the past will start fading. Watch carefully how oil is traded.

- Coal mining is also an indicator of growth. A slowing in coal production or increase in coal prices indicates economic decrease.

- Watch how fast-food chains prosper or close operations. This is a true test of economic health, especially in a fast-food nation like America. A time will come when we will not have access to quick and easy everything. In every nation, the ultimate fight will be over food and water.

- Watch defaults on national loans in other countries, which will affect many other nations.

- China will start manipulating the resources of many nations. China now accounts for more global trade than any other nation, and the Chinese are able to manipulate any world market. Their trade power will increase and be used as a point of control in days ahead.

Financial rule is shifting in the world around us. Satan will use this to manipulate and wear down the saints.

I feel that many people's spirits have been vexed and broken by mammon, such that they have lost strength to wage a good fight for their inheritance. Therefore, I am decreeing a revival of the spirit of man! We are entering into a time of revival of the spirit of man, the innermost part of a person, where the Holy Spirit resides. The spirit of man sings and blesses God. Ask the Lord to release your spirit from any vexation so you can bless the Lord. Get past your wounds and confinements and let your spirit bless God. Let Him touch you in a way He has never touched you before. Tell the Lord you are willing, that you want wholeness, that you want Him to transform your blood and remove any impurities from your life. Be willing to overthrow iniquitous structures in your family bloodline. Overturn your "father's altar of worship" and enter a new way for victory in your life in the days ahead.

Overthrowing Cycles and Unraveling the Cord

As we prepare for a new level of freedom, we must deal with forces that wish to keep us captive in an old season. This is a time to break destructive cycles. A cycle is a periodically repeated sequence of events, something that happens over and over at a certain time. It can be linked with a time or an event and orchestrated supernaturally so that a repeating wound or injustice occurs from generation to generation. Satan loves to keep us going around the same mountain. But God has a remedy for iniquity—by embracing the blood and redemptive sacrifice of the Lord Jesus Christ, we can break out of any old pattern.

We have looked at how poverty attempts to create a stronghold to keep us from seeing our prosperity. The third force in the three-fold cord of religion empowered by mammon to produce a poverty mentality is infirmity. Infirmity encompasses more than just sickness and disease; it is also related to suffering and sorrow. Matthew 8:16–17 states that Jesus "cast out the spirits with a word, and healed all who were sick, that it might be fulfilled which was spoken by Isaiah the prophet, saying: 'He Himself took our infirmities and bore our sicknesses.'" (See also Isaiah 53:4.) Infirmity can also refer to a disability of one kind or another. It can occur as a result of moral or spiritual defects that cause our will to stray from God, and it can be caused by the influence of an evil spirit (as in Luke 13:11–16).

Infirmity can also be linked to overall weakness in our bodies or with anything that creates weakness, such as grief. Romans 15:1 (NASB) states that those "who are strong ought to bear the weaknesses of those without strength." This weakness is infirmity. Not only did Christ bear our weaknesses and infirmities, we are also called to bear the weaknesses and infirmities of our brothers and sisters in the Lord. This is called "intercession." Romans 8:26 (KJV) says, "Likewise the Spirit also helpeth our infirmities: for we know not what we should pray for as we ought: but the Spirit itself maketh intercession for us with groanings which cannot be uttered." We have been called to intercede for the sick, which allows us to bring before the Lord someone weaker than ourselves.

A Generational Understanding

Infirmity can be a generational issue, though people are often confused about how generational iniquity works.[2] To fully understand generational iniquity, we need to first understand how DNA serves as the blueprint of our bodies by causing traits from one generation to be passed to the next. As the cells in an embryo divide and multiply, they do so according to the sequence of base pairs in DNA. The combination of these base pairs provides the hereditary instructions for constructing each cell in order to accomplish that cell's specific purpose. As cells continue to multiply, groups of cells come together to form tissues; tissues, in turn, form organs. Each cell, tissue and organ has a specific function. Blood cells are pumped through the body, providing oxygen needed for survival to each organ. The cells in our stomachs coordinate in the process of digestion. The cells in our brains work together to store memories as we study and pursue knowledge.

When the sperm and egg unite and a new life is formed, already programmed into the makeup of that person is God's redemptive plan. We must remember, however, that we are born in iniquity, so the iniquitous inherited traits that will resist God's plan are also already programmed in us. Our blood begins to war with itself from the time of conception. Since cells are dynamic, an iniquitous pattern in a cell's DNA can affect our entire physical and mental makeup. If something is passed on in our DNA that has been twisted or linked with iniquity, that message is multiplied wrongly in our beings.

But God! The Spirit of God can come into our lives so that we become sons of God (Galatians 3:26). As we submit and yield our lives to the Spirit's work, He flows through our blood and cleanses our consciences from the thought processes linked with iniquitous patterns in our bloodlines. Hebrews 9:14 (NIV) states, "How much more, then, will the blood of Christ, who through the eternal Spirit offered himself unblemished to God, cleanse our consciences from acts that lead to death, so that we may serve the living God!"

The Lord had to show me generational infirmity in my life by His Spirit. In my case, a generational weakness had aligned itself with loss and trauma. *But God!* Once I saw those weaknesses and defined the losses that they were attached to, I could then pray and break a power that had me bent over. I confessed those patterns as sin. You might say, "But you had nothing to do with these sins!" We must understand that repentance is a gift and grace of God that causes us to turn from one way of thinking and be transformed to think like Christ. Once you repent, you renounce the power of its effect. In my life, this set me on a new road to health.

Trusted doctors and praying friends have helped me greatly. Each doctor played his role in diagnosing my condition. It was the Spirit of God, however, that changed me from the inside. He is there now to reveal things to you and show you how weakness and loss are related.

Press Through and *See* His Power

I wish I could say that I have never been sick again since I started seeing how infirmity works with loss and trauma. Even so, since that time a power to resist sickness has become resident within me. When the power of infirmity comes against me, I submit to God, resist the devil and watch him flee.

Healing sick people was one of Jesus' major ministries. He dealt with many organic causes of illness and with individuals affected by madness, birth defects and infections. The blind, the deaf, the lame and others who suffered approached Him for help. I especially love the story of the woman with the spirit of infirmity who "pressed through" in Mark 5:25–34. She is an incredible example of personal overcoming. She overcame the religious structure of the day, the reproach of being a woman and the stigma of being unclean. She pressed through to touch the Lord, causing Him to release "virtue" from His own body, as it is translated in the King James Version ("power" in the New King James Version), which healed her condition.

In the Hebraic culture, most people believed that illness was the direct consequence of sin. Jesus shifted this concept by healing a blind man who had been sick since birth in John 9. When Jesus' disciples asked, "Who sinned, this man or his parents, that he was born blind?" (verse 2), Jesus answered that the sickness was not related to the man or his parents, "but that the works of God should be revealed in him" (verse 3). Many wrong choices produce consequences in our bodies, but Jesus came to extend grace to bring us out from bondage to the punishment of sin and into healing and wholeness. He had the power to both forgive sin and to heal (see Matthew 9:1–8; compare Mark 2:1–12; Luke 5:17–26).

On several occasions Jesus used His own saliva as an ointment or anointing (Mark 7:32–35; 8:22–25; John 9:6–7). I find this fascinating, because one of the primary ways that DNA is collected for testing is through saliva samples. Jesus took His own saliva, placed it on the eyes of the blind and watched their eyes transform. He also healed those who suffered from mental illnesses and epilepsy, sicknesses usually associated with demonic powers (Mark 9:17–18). The Lord addressed issues of fever and dysentery (Matthew 8:14–15). Sterility and barrenness were also major issues in biblical times. Regardless of the cause of their distress, people found that Jesus could truly help. He is there for you. Be like the woman in Mark 5 and "press through" all the structures stopping you from experiencing freedom and *seeing* a new wholeness and peace that are waiting for you.

God is creating a strong people who are not afraid of the war ahead. Satan will attempt to braid together a three-fold cord against you. Not only can you unravel this cord, but the cord can become a "rope of hope" for the future. We will triumph!

10

What Will Become of Me?

As you can see, we are approaching an incredible season in our abode of earth! If you are a blood-bought believer of Jesus of Nazareth, through His blood and by His Spirit you have already been repositioned. We walk in this earth, but we live in heavenly places, for He has ascended and we are seated next to Him (see Ephesians 1:20–21; 2:6). Therefore, we are *already* beyond this world and should think with an eternal perspective. Though we are in time, time does not fully control us. On the other hand, our enemy's operations are limited to time and laws of nature and the spiritual realm. We must recognize the manipulation in our adversary's works. In the midst of his distractions, however, we must also remember that, like our Lord who was called to destroy the works of the enemy, we are called to do the same (1 John 3:8).

As I begin this last chapter, I want to emphasize that by revelation I know that we triumph in the end. Our dear friend Penny Jackson is our houseguest during conferences and special family events. She is a seasoned teacher who likes answers. In the midst of our discussions of Scripture, books and doctrines of the "end times," Penny voices that question most people have: "What will become of me?" She wants to know how the situation will affect her so she can adjust her life accordingly.

Deep in our hearts we all want to know what will become of us. We have heard many theories and doctrines about the end of the world, so it is a valid question. I also believe that we choose how to view the future. As I have said, future is linked with expectation, and expectation is tied to our emotions. Therefore, thinking about events to come can bring dread, fear or hope.

There are still several questions to be answered: What will we look like in days ahead? What will we have to go through? How will we gather? How will we advance? What will our real mission look like? What level of unity and agreement must we flow in? How will our supply lines be released? I will try to answer these using knowledge of the Word and prophetic insight God has given me.

Which Church Am I?

One of the most read and least understood books in the Bible is Revelation. Each year I try to read this book aloud, because the first chapter gives the promise of a blessing from God for those who will read the book. One year, I took a team to Patmos Island, where we read the entire book near the place where the Lord visited John and revealed the end times. Recently, in a corporate prayer gathering, we read a chapter each day out loud and prayed from the incredible richness of the life contained in the words.

The book of Revelation provides deep insight into the nature and tactics of the enemy. The supernatural visitation came to John during an extreme time of persecution. In the midst of it, he saw that the Lord God omnipotent reigns! He seemed to agree with Paul that those who follow the Lord in their daily lives will enter into and be involved in continuing spiritual conflict, and in Revelation we find much strategy on how to stay in a hidden place with the Lord, and how to go to war in alignment with the saints. In the book of Revelation we find the dragon, the Beast, the harlot of Babylon, the false prophet, the Antichrist and many other of Satan's followers. We find the accuser of the brethren accusing us day and night. Needless to say, the book is quite important. I find many, however, with the same thought that Penny expresses: *What will become of me?*

Revelation has been given to us like a set of keys to unlock victory during times of darkness and distress. One key theme is vibrant praise and worship. Another is found in the first chapter, in which John sees a vision of seven golden lampstands. In context, I believe these are seven menorahs—that is, seven *seven-branched* lampstands. The Lord then tells John that these seven lampstands represent seven churches.

What are the seven churches? First, we know that they were literal churches that existed in John's day in the Roman province of Asia. But it is clear that these churches were not chosen at random; they are called *the* seven churches. In some way, these seven churches represent *all* of the Church!

Some have suggested that they represent seven eras of Church history: Each church depicts a different historical time period, beginning with Ephesus as the earliest Church and ending with lukewarm Laodicea as the Church today. The problem with that interpretation is that it does not work. It might sound convincing to Christians living in America, where many churches match the description of the lukewarm Laodiceans. But the American Church is only a fraction of the Church worldwide. In places such as China and Africa, major segments of the Church are filled with life and power in the midst of severe persecution. The fact is that the majority of the Church today is not Laodicean.

I believe a better explanation is that the churches in Revelation represent seven *kinds* of churches. These church types exist in every time period, although at certain times and in certain places, one will tend to be more representative than the others. That means every church, and every Christian, is to be found among these seven churches. In them we see the strategies Satan uses to keep God's people from fulfilling their call. But we also hear God's heart concerning the Church, as Jesus walks among the lampstands, tending to each one, and offers instructions on how they can burn brightly. (The appendix, "An Analysis of the Seven Churches of Revelation," can help you identify where you stand spiritually.)[1]

Gaining an understanding of the churches in Revelation is vital if we are to continue praying for transformation in our regions. The seven churches represent regions, for which they serve as menorah lights. Each has an array of characteristics, some good, some bad. That is why the Lord commended each church and revealed weak points that needed to be addressed.

When I cannot hear God or revelation seems to be blocked, I have learned to do two things. First, I always ask God what I should give, for when I follow His pattern of giving, faith begins to rise and I can see what I need to see. Second, I read John's revelation to the seven churches and ask God, *What church am I?* If I am in intercession, I also ask, *What church am I dealing with?* This points me to my lampstand first to see if it is burning brightly. Just as we must deal with our brother's sin by first examining our own shortcomings (Matthew 7:3–5), so it is when we search for a reason behind the absence of His voice or revelation. This also allows me to see how powerful the fire is burning in the atmosphere of the group with which I am worshiping. I always feel that the group or ministry where I have been assigned reflects one of the churches of Revelation, and this gives me great insight on how to pray.

Come Up Here!

One of my favorite verses in all of the Bible is Revelation 4:1–2:

> After these things I looked, and behold, a door standing open in heaven. And the first voice which I heard was like a trumpet speaking with me, saying, "Come up here, and I will show you things which must take place after this." Immediately I was in the Spirit; and behold, a throne set in heaven, and One sat on the throne.

After He had dealt with the regional church structure in chapters 2–3, the Lord opened a door through which we see what lies beyond where we are presently worshiping in earth. This door into heaven causes faith to soar, and faith overcomes!

The shield of faith is closely related to the concept of a door—the Greek term for shield being *thureos*, from *thura*, a square shield that can be seen as a door. The door is used symbolically in the Bible in many ways: For example, the Valley of Achor, a place of trouble in Joshua 7:26, is later promised as "a door of hope" in Hosea 2:15. It will become a reason for God's people to trust Him again. Our trouble can be turned into an entry point into a new place of victory.

Jesus called Himself "the door" (John 10:7, 9). Faith in Him is the only way to enter the Kingdom of God. God gave to the Gentiles "the door of faith" (Acts 14:27), an opportunity to know Him as Lord. Jesus stands at the door and knocks (Revelation 3:20). He calls all people to Himself, but He will not enter without permission. We need to give the Lord permission to take us through new, opportune doors and to allow Him to enter and give us power to go through these doors.

Dutch Sheets also had a revelation of the door into the heavenly places. As I wrote in chapter 6, he and I visited every state in the United States to mobilize intercessors across the nation. Dutch wrote that the Lord had begun preparing him for it by having him read the five references to "heavenly places" in Ephesians as a unit:

> Blessed be the God and Father of our Lord Jesus Christ, who has blessed us with every spiritual blessing in the heavenly places in Christ . . . which He worked in Christ when He raised Him from the dead and seated Him at His right hand in the heavenly places . . . and raised us up together, and made us sit together in the heavenly places in Christ Jesus . . . to the intent that now the manifold wisdom of God might be made known by the church to the principalities and powers in the heavenly places . . . For we do not wrestle against flesh and blood, but against principalities, against powers, against the rulers of the darkness of this age, against spiritual hosts of wickedness in the heavenly places.
>
> Ephesians 1:3, 20; 2:6; 3:10; 6:12

Dutch writes,

> Taken together, these power-packed verses reveal several important things about operating in the invisible realm of the spirit. First of all, the Lord informs us that we have been given everything we need to operate in this arena. He then states that Christ has been positioned there with all authority, and we who have been seated there with Him, share in this authority. This is followed by a declaration that we, the Church, will manifest God's great wisdom to the opposing forces that operate there. And finally, in the last reference, the Holy Spirit identifies these invisible enemies that we will overcome by using God's wisdom, power, and authority. Amazing![2]

On this journey, Dutch shared that the most literal rendering of Matthew 16:19 is as follows: "And I will give thee the keys of the Kingdom of heavens [plural]. And whatever thou shalt bind on the earth shall be as having been bound in the heavens [plural]; and whatever thou shalt loose on the earth shall be as having been loosed in the heavens [plural]."[3] Notice that Jesus was not referring to heaven where God's throne is but to the spiritual realm around us. He was speaking of our involvement and responsibility in it. The two verses describe the Church as having authority (keys) to govern for Christ in the heavens—the invisible realm of the spirit—while on earth. And He promised us that when we do, the powers of hell would not overpower us.

Dutch continued to share:

> The Holy Spirit led me to yet another passage, Micah 2:13 (NAS): "The breaker goes up before them; they break out, pass through the gate and go out by it. So their king goes on before them, and the Lord at their head." . . . What the Holy Spirit finally zeroed me in on was the little word "up"

(Hebrew—*alah*), which means to ascend or rise up. I finally realized what the Holy Spirit was endeavoring to say to me: *We must follow Christ, the Breaker, up into the heavenly places, so we can partner with Him and experience breakthrough there. Breaking through in the invisible realm of the spirit always creates breakthrough in the visible, natural realm.*[4]

The Door Is Up Here

Connecting heaven and earth releases the glory of God into our realm. The release of God's glory is no small thing! Moses cried out for it in Exodus 33:18, "Show me Your glory!" (NASB). The word in Hebrew is *kabowd*, which means "weighty or heavy." Glory signifies authority. The word can also mean wealthy or prosperous, from the sense of being heavy with goods. When heaven and earth connect, releasing God's glory, His weighty presence is felt and great authority is released.

The New Testament word for glory, *doxa*, has in its root meaning the recognition of something—or someone—for what it really is. When the glory of the Lord is released, He is recognized! Saints and sinners will recognize Him, and His weighty presence will change things. A bold people will wear this glory. I think the greatest war ahead is in this realm. The enemy knows that if God's people wear His glory, the moving ark of His presence in them will dethrone Satan, just as the Ark of the Covenant toppled Dagon.

Paul, who constantly sought open doors of service that enabled him to minister in the name of Jesus Christ, wrote, "For a great and effective door has opened to me, and there are many adversaries" (1 Corinthians 16:9). Doors of opportunity lie ahead of each of us, but the adversaries behind those doors will overtake us unless our door of faith is in place. As I said earlier, our shield of faith is really a door. Lift it up!

We need not be afraid to venture into new places where the Lord leads us. Though many adversaries stand in our paths, our shield of faith will quench their fiery darts. Jeremiah 46:3 (NIV) is encouraging: "Prepare your shields, both large and small, and march out for battle!" Let us go forth with confidence, with our shields lifted high, and our victory will be assured.

It is time to break through, rise up and advance into a new movement that rearranges history. This is a time for us to "be" the people we read about in Revelation. Many new doors of harvest will open in days ahead. We must be ready to go through, defy the enemy and release what has been captive to come back under God's rule and authority.

Sound Connects Heaven and Earth

The book of Revelation reveals the future age of the Tabernacle of David, and it reflects how heaven is filled with sound. In Revelation 4, the triumphant people arise and we "see" the worship in heaven and the call to God's army on earth to boldly enter. The great move of God arising in the world will begin with sound. The tribe of Judah had to go first for victory to be secured in the Promised Land, and God's pattern does not change. The apostolic, governing tribe, who knew how to use sound to win wars, had to remain creative to be victorious. Sound creates movement.

We recently hosted a corporate gathering in which we focused solely on praise. We decreed that God's Kingdom people would arise with a new strength and new sound. We asked the Lord to open a portal of divine revelation for the next season. This portal would connect heaven with earth and cause people to rise up in a new triumphant movement. While we were praying, we could feel a new level of God's presence entering the atmosphere. I have faith that we will see this manifest in days to come.

Our Finest Hour Is Coming

Peter Wagner, a hero in the faith, seems to fully analyze what the Body is going through. His "paradigm language" helps us better define the changes that many are embracing over what they believe. In his book *This Changes Everything*, he shares the following:

> The major change in my personal paradigm shift was to look toward the future and believe that the power of God is active, the Kingdom of God is advancing, and the people of God are being prepared for their finest hour. Satan has had too much dominion over this earth for too long a time. . . . Jesus first came to earth and died on the cross to destroy the works of the devil, and this passage [1 Corinthians 15:24] concerning the end times affirms that before it is all over, Jesus will have finished whatever it takes to destroy the works of the devil. This has not happened as yet. It is still sometime in the future.
>
> Revelation 11.15 records the words of the seventh angel: "The kingdoms of this world have become the kingdoms of our Lord." Remember Jesus' third temptation, when Satan offered to give Him all the kingdoms of the world (see Matthew 4:8–9)? It was a legitimate offer because at that time Satan still had dominion over all the kingdoms. However, Jesus then died on the cross, rose again and gave the power of the Holy Spirit to His disciples in order to complete His Great Commission of making disciples of all the nations. Revelation 11:15 shows that by the end times, this will literally

have happened. Satan will no longer rule; instead, "He [Jesus] shall reign forever and ever!"

In Acts 3:21, Apostle Peter is speaking to a crowd after he and John had healed the lame man at the temple gate . . . [and] speaks of Jesus, "whom heaven must receive until . . ." Until when? Heaven had just received Jesus, but for how long? Jesus came to the earth once, but when would He come back? This is one of the most important eschatological questions of all, and Peter gives us the answer: "until the times of restoration of all things."

This is worth looking into for a moment. Jesus came to reconcile the world, which Satan had usurped from Adam, back to the Father. He gave the ministry, or the implementation, of that reconciliation to us, His disciples. Since Jesus died on the cross, huge progress has been made. The world and the quality of life of the human race is much better now than it was 2,000 years ago. One day the restoration of all things will be completed, but that day has not yet come. Jesus is still in heaven. Do you think He could come today? Not if we take this Scripture at face value, because all things have not yet been restored. This is one of the compelling reasons why I have found my old paradigm of futurist eschatology deficient.

This is my opinion:

- We do not need a defeatist eschatology; we need a victorious eschatology.
- We do not need a negative eschatology; we need a positive eschatology.
- We do not need an escapist eschatology; we need a dominion eschatology.
- We do not need a passive eschatology; we need an active eschatology.[5]

I agree with the concept of *victorious eschatology* and embrace Peter's choice for us to become active and triumphant in our thinking, though I see this more from a prophetic perspective than through a teacher's interpretation. We have not experienced all the war necessary for us to see the fullness of Christ's plan. Because the Church has refused to mature and put away naïve ways of thinking, great wars and conflicts lie before us, particularly a major war with the accuser of the brethren.

Revelation 10:4–7 says,

> Now when the seven thunders uttered their voices, I was about to write; but I heard a voice from heaven saying to me, "Seal up the things which the seven thunders uttered, and do not write them." The angel whom I saw standing on the sea and on the land raised up his hand to heaven and swore by Him who lives forever and ever, who created heaven and the things that are in it, the earth and the things that are in it, and the sea and the things that are in it, that there should be delay no longer, but in the days of the sounding of the seventh angel, when he is about to sound, the mystery of God would be finished, as He declared to His servants the prophets.

Some prophetic knowledge and revelation has been locked up for times to come. I believe as the Church moves with apostolic, prophetic authority, this revelation unlocks. I also see war intensifying over the land of Israel. Therefore, for all of God's Kingdom children, war will intensify. I have never believed that we could escape what is ahead, so I have chosen to develop a triumphant way of thinking about the future.

We Choose to Be Victorious

Peter Wagner gives us four areas in which we can choose to think victoriously. My wife, Pam, saw another in a dream.

Pam is practical and approaches life with a functional goal, and her dream helps us see our choices in an apocalyptic setting[6]:

I was in a post-apocalyptic world in which a third of the human population had been wiped out by some sort of pestilence. The survivors knew that half of us would die and half would live. Because of the massive loss of life, the world's infrastructure had collapsed, and it was every man for himself. The group I was with found an abandoned grocery store on the edge of a ridge overlooking a valley and began to stock up on provisions.

Once inside, I realized that my mother- and father-in-law's house was next door. They were no longer living in the house, but I knew that weapons and ammunition were inside. I also knew that its water supply was contaminated, so we brought all the bottled water from the store, along with any other nonperishable food and supplies, into the house. We knew we would have to establish our headquarters in that house and wait out the coming devastation.

During this time of preparation, I was aware that some people were making decisions about their fate. Because they knew half of the remaining people would die from the pestilence, they took things from the grocery store that could be used to end their lives in the event that they were stricken by disease or they faced the opposition that had already killed a third of humanity. They refused to suffer through the symptoms and determined to take things into their own hands.[7]

This dream contains many interesting choices: Each person had to choose (1) to find supply, (2) hope over defeatism, (3) to continue living life, (4) to suffer to triumph, (5) to see beyond his or her circumstances and (6) to overcome death. My parents' house was available but unoccupied, which says that one generation is fading and a new generation must learn to use the weapons they have inherited and create new weapons for new wars.

Notice the activation of will that is necessary to choose one's future. Just as Peter Wagner made a choice to move into victory, in her dream Pam had to choose to triumph in the midst of adverse circumstances.

In July 2004, I had a dream that has influenced my thinking. God showed me a barn and storehouse, and suddenly many scorpions appeared. The Lord said, *Eat the scorpions!*, so I did and got rid of them. Then I proceeded toward the barn. On each side of the walkway were four snakes, hybrid creatures like cobras with rattlesnake bodies. The Lord spoke again: *The enemy is uniting and becoming a hybrid. To get in the storehouse, you will have to get past the snakes.* But I did not know how to deal with them, so I turned around and walked away.

I felt defeated by the dream, but God was not finished with me; each year I have gained revelation as I have pondered it. First, I turned around because I knew that there was no antidote for hybrid snakebites. Some hybrid breeds cannot be combated. Recently when sharing the dream, I also heard the part about *Eat the scorpions!* Scorpion venom is actually used as a medical treatment. God had already prepared me to get past the snakes by ingesting the scorpions, but I was ignorant to the antidote I already had within me. This dream also reveals the presence of great storehouses that need to be opened up but are being guarded by clusters of enemies from hell. These enemies will create fear to convince us that they are too strong for us to pass. Choose to go past what is guarding the supply for your future.

Satan looks for the most opportune time to inflict pain on God's children. We need to understand how demon forces will confederate in an attempt to steal the inheritance of the Lord. We find this in 2 Chronicles 20 when Jehoshaphat had to face three armies who had aligned as one. Witchcraft will align with the accuser of the brethren to tear down from within what God is building. Witchcraft joining with the power of the dragon's fire is a deadly force. The dragon is that serpent force that opposes the Bride. The power of the enemy confronting the Church causes the serpent Leviathan to use communication lines to control many who are willing to listen.

In 2 Chronicles 20, the people of Judah won the war because they listened to the prophet that arose during the crisis. That prophet told them where to go and what to do. Victory came when they used sound, and in the future there will be a new expression of sound. A new sound is an element of surprise to the enemy. Changing your sound produces a fresh weapon and a tool for building and advancing the Kingdom. This also holds true for movement (dance). If we will stand and worship, the enemy will go into confusion.

Just as Nehemiah returned to build a city that had been abandoned for seventy years, the Lord is raising up a divine return of His people to occupy lands and cultures of society. Only a Kingdom people who worship the King of Kings can present harvested nations to Him. God is concerned about the worship of His people from nation to nation throughout the earth. "The earth is the LORD's, and the fulness thereof" (Psalm 24:1 KJV).

In a prophetic ministry like Glory of Zion International, we have many dreamers. Klancy Cunningham usually brings dream revelation to most prayer gatherings. Her dream below depicts our identity in days ahead.

243

I found myself under a dome or a huge bubble, which I believe kept things hidden or protected. I saw soldiers—men, women, youth and children—in rank and file, but the army was very unusual. All soldiers were wearing beautiful turquoise shirts, but they were more like tunics. On each tunic was embroidered the ephod stones. It looked like moveable fabric, but when you touched it, it turned into a breastplate. The helmets they wore looked more like crowns or a cross between helmet and crown. The shields on their backs were of a reflective gold that would blind you when the sun bounced off it. The swords by their side had *HOLY* etched down the blade. To the right of each person sat a huge lion on his haunches. Hanging from his neck was a shofar engraved in gold and silver. Two angels in battle gear stood with each individual, one behind each person and one to the left. The angel to the left had *USURPER* etched across his breastplate; the one behind had *JUDGMENT* etched on his breastplate. They looked fierce and somber, but I sensed anticipation, too, as though they knew a day was coming that they had long been preparing for.[8]

The War over Life

Despite what the media and culture say, the ultimate war of our times is not about oil, land or nuclear power. Nor is it about terrorism or homeland security. The real war concerns one thing: *life.* God places each of us in a specific time and space where we are meant to experience life to its fullest. Acts 17:24–27 puts it this way:

> God, who made the world and everything in it, since He is Lord of heaven and earth, does not dwell in temples made with hands. Nor is He worshiped with men's hands, as though He needed anything, since He gives to all life, breath, and all things. And He has made from one blood

every nation of men to dwell on all the face of the earth, and has determined their preappointed times and the boundaries of their dwellings, so that they should seek the Lord, in the hope that they might grope for Him and find Him, though He is not far from each one of us.

He has a perfect time and place determined for you, where you can "grope for Him and find Him." When you grab hold of God, you can bring His blessings into the earth realm. Old cycles break; restoration brings you full circle into God's perfect plan. God does not look at how long sin or iniquity has been in place; He looks for someone who will grab hold of Him and start His process working in the earth. To "grope" means to touch God. When we touch God and He touches us, heaven and earth come into agreement and covenant blessings are released.

Process is the course of development and eventual coming into full operation. It includes preparation, discipline, order, change, development and operational steps that bring you to a destination. In this age we must fight to keep those God-appointed times and boundaries. Each day we live is a life-or-death matter. That sounds dramatic, but it is true. Every day we fight against forces that seek to steal pieces of our existence bit by bit. Some days the battle seems minor; on others we war for our very next breath.

Our culture would have us believe that life can be compartmentalized—some areas are worth dying for, others can be neglected if they do not meet our criteria of moral importance. This is why people who fight for environmentalism, stem cell research or human rights can justify abortion. We value life—when it is convenient for us.

Life involves the whole person. It is not just our physical surroundings or our emotional well-being. For every human being, life is a spiritual matter. Natural life has a beginning but no real end. By that I mean that our Maker has established us as eternal beings. Yes, our natural bodies will pass away like the withering of the trees. But our spiritual beings will remain. What we believe and how we stand firm on behalf of our faith will carry on just as it does for the people in Hebrews 11. Those men and women did not do everything correctly, but they left a legacy of faith!

What Will Your Legacy Be?

Let me tell a story about a man familiar to most of you. You know him as a traitor, but he could have been a hero if he had dealt with the bitterness and trauma in his life. There are probably many in the world like Benedict Arnold.

In the first year of the American Revolution, morale in the Continental army was low. The British were so successful at driving the American army back from New York City, through New Jersey and into Pennsylvania that the British buglers began to use the tune for "A Hunting We Shall Go" instead of the normal call for *charge*.

The British planned to divide and conquer by bringing their northern army south from Canada to separate New England from the middle and southern colonies. Standing in their way was Horatio Gates, commander of the Continental army in upstate New York. Though an experienced officer, Gates was arrogant and ambitious and not above underhanded attempts to seize George Washington's job, which he believed was rightfully his. His battle strategies were always slow and cautious, earning him the nickname "Granny Gates." He also frequently snubbed his junior officers and, worse, took credit for their achievements.

One of those junior officers was a young man named Benedict Arnold, one of the army's most capable and experienced young commanders. A brilliant war strategist and natural leader, he repeatedly found victory in impossible assignments through his iron will and innovation. Tasked with stopping the British fleet as they sailed down Lake Champlain on the New York and Vermont border, he built a makeshift navy out of men who were not sailors and ships made of green timbers that warped and leaked. Yet he succeeded in repelling perhaps the strongest navy in the world.

In 1777, as the British southward offensive culminated on a battlefield in Saratoga, New York, Arnold recognized a weak place in the American line that the British could exploit. He petitioned Gates to let him move that part of the line into an offensive operation, but Granny Gates preferred the safer defensive position. The argument between the two escalated until Gates relieved Arnold of his command. When the battle ensued, Arnold could not long endure hearing the guns and watching the smoke rising from the weak spot. He raced into the fray to find the British breaking through the weak point. Arnold raced up and down the battlefield, rallying the disorganized troops and sending them back into the breach. The battle turned and the British were forced into retreat and eventual surrender.

Saratoga became the turning point of the American Revolution. Britain was shocked by the capture of their entire northern army and were forced to take the Americans seriously. The French now felt confident to enter the war with their much needed money, supplies and troops. American morale soared as they saw that they could indeed beat the British on the battlefield. And credit for the victory went to . . . Granny Gates, who claimed it in his report to

Washington and the Continental Congress. It was not the first time Arnold had been robbed of the credit due him. Though a great commander, Arnold was not apt at petty politics and had several times been passed over for promotion in lieu of a less competent but politically connected candidate.

Sadly, Benedict Arnold could not overcome his bitterness at his treatment, and he allowed that bitterness to bring forth the fruit of treason for which he is now remembered more than two hundred years later, such that his name is synonymous with the word *traitor*. If he had overcome his acrimony, trauma and bitterness, he could have been forever known as the man who turned the battle that turned the war and won a nation's freedom.

In this season we could go either way, with the Lord or against Him. I call these the "fine line times"—we must choose this day whom we will serve.

The Call to Enjoy Life

The war we fight is not only over our very existence but the manner of life we live. How we live in the place and time in which we have been established determines our manner of life. Satan wants to keep us in poverty and infirmity, to relegate our spiritual existence to barren religion. He wants to steal every ounce of joy and purpose we have. If it were up to him, we would never know abundance, health or freedom in worship. *But God!* Our Maker has a destiny in Him for us. Jesus expresses this in John 10:10: "I have come that they may have life, and that they may have it more abundantly." Considering that we live in a time of war, is this abundance even possible? And if so, how?

War is violent, evoking ideas of artillery and bloodshed. By the same token, we are called by God to be violent in the spirit realm: "And from the days of John the Baptist until now the kingdom of heaven suffers violence, and the violent take it by force" (Matthew 11:12). How are we to be violent in the Spirit? In the mist of the battle, we must not lose the joy of life! If we lose joy, then we lose the strength necessary to birth our future.

We must learn to praise our way through every obstacle. Merely declaring the name of God causes a violent reaction from the enemy. When we praise, we yield a mighty weapon in heavenly places. We are living in violent times, so praise violently! My dictionary defines *violence* as a "vehement, forcible, or destructive action, often involving infringement, outrage, or assault." We are to be violent with our praise, assaulting and destroying the works of the enemy in the process. Talk about warfare!

There is more to the revelation of violent praise. *Praise* comes from a Latin word meaning "value" or "price." To give praise to God is to proclaim His merit or worth in every situation. You can shout, "Glory," release blessing and express heartfelt thanksgiving. God will enthrone Himself in the midst of our circumstances, and He will take on any strategy the enemy uses to bind, block and captivate us.

Praise can be given through many means, as long as it is a natural heart expression and not an outward show (Matthew 15:8). The most common expression in a modern-day church setting is through music, both instrumental and vocal (Psalm 150:3–5). Paul specifically mentions singing psalms, hymns and spiritual songs in the corporate worship setting (Colossians 3:16). Yet worshiping warriors know there are many other everyday ways to declare the name of the

Lord: offering sacrifices (Leviticus 7:13), physical movement (2 Samuel 6:14), silence and meditation (Psalm 77:11–12), testimony (Psalm 66:16), prayer (Philippians 4:6) and living a holy life (1 Peter 1:3–9). Praise also includes spontaneous outbursts of thanksgiving in response to a redemptive act of God (Exodus 15; Judges 5; 1 Samuel 2; Luke 1:46–55, 67–79). Each of these expressions of praise can become violent when you are determined to advance in God's Kingdom plan.

One final note concerning praise: In seasons of war, many of us have gone through various trials so that we could learn how to bring God's victorious sound from heaven into our atmosphere. How we establish this atmosphere of victory sets our course for the future. This is a season of victorious sound. Keep in mind that new songs and sounds will break old cycles and cause us to advance, enlarge and define our boundaries. God's sound permeates from heaven and orders much of what goes on in the earthly realm. When He is ready to bring restoration to earth, He releases His sound. And Scripture repeatedly indicates that Judah, meaning "praise," goes first. Who leads this praise? No less than Christ, the Lion of Judah (Revelation 5:5). The Lion of Judah roars! As ambassadors of Christ, that roar of God is within us.

Amos 3:8 tells us that when the roar of the Lord goes forth, a prophetic mantle falls. Joel 2:28 paints a picture of what this covering looks like: "Your sons and your daughters shall prophesy, your old men shall dream dreams, your young men shall see visions." The Spirit of the Lord longs to be voiced through such a prophetic mantle. Let that begin with the roar of the Lord announcing both His arrival and His praise. As you shake off passivity and roar with a holy roar, allow the Lord to loose those things that lie deep within you. Let Him break hidden grief that has kept your joy capped. Open the gates for Him to release blessings from within.

Change the Atmosphere and Occupy the Land

Praise literally creates a different atmosphere around us because the Lord comes down and inhabits our worship (Psalm 22:3). The God of the universe dwells in the midst of our praising Him. It is not hard to imagine, then, why this changes our measure of faith and gives us strength to grab hold of the inheritance He has for us.

Did you know that you have a portion specifically allotted to you from God? The word *inheritance* means "my portion." We all have a portion. We have all been given a space, territory or arena in which we have been granted authority. How we steward that space is key to our success in the spirit realm. In fact, the climate of our domain reflects our relationship with the Lord. Therefore, our chief desire should be for the presence of the Holy God to occupy our inheritance. In Deuteronomy 1:8 and 8:1, we read,

> See, I have set the land before you; go in and possess the land which the LORD swore to your fathers—to Abraham, Isaac, and Jacob—to give to them and their descendants after them. . . . Every commandment which I command you today you must be careful to observe, that you may live and multiply, and go in and possess the land of which the LORD swore to your fathers.

In warring against the enemies of this age, we must learn how to occupy and possess. When we occupy something, we take possession of it or keep it in our possession. In Luke 21:19 we are called to posses our souls. When we possess the portion that God has for each of us, we become whole, ful-filled and full of peace. This is what we are actually warring to accomplish! We must be a people who settle for nothing less than the abundance the Lord has for us.

Recently, when I was reviewing Scripture in the Ampli-fied version in preparation to speak, I read John 10:10, a Scripture that has sustained me through my life (emphasis added): "The thief comes only in order to steal and kill and destroy. I came that they may *have* and *enjoy* life, and have it in abundance [to the full, till it overflows]."

I had written an entire book on that Scripture, when I read it that day, for the first time I understood something I had never really grasped before. He came that we may have and *enjoy* life! The thief actually comes to destroy the joy of life. If we recognize this, we will always have the strength to overcome him.

An Interesting Season of Signs

The prophetic significance of the four lunar eclipses occur-ring on Jewish biblical feast days in 2014–2015 became a focus on the Internet and in best sellers throughout the world. Are the "blood moons" really significant regarding the Jewish people and the so-called end times? Are we entering inter-national times of severe judgment known as "the day of the Lord"? Is the darkening of sun, moon and stars approach-ing, and will the moon turn blood red? Will there be a full anti-Jewish military invasion of Israel? Will the heavens and earth shake with worldwide earthquakes of unprecedented magnitude and overwhelming floods?

God "made the moon *to mark the seasons*, and the sun knows when to go down" (Psalm 104:19 NIV, emphasis added).

The changing of seasons and feast times are denoted by the moon. The Scriptures also have many helpful things to say about heavenly signs and the moon specifically (see Isaiah 13:9–11; 24:21–23; Ezekiel 32:7–8; Joel 2:10–12, 28–32; 3:12–17; Matthew 24:29–30; Acts 2:12–21; and Revelation 6:12–16). We can watch the moon or worship it; I have chosen to watch.

Blood moons signify a change in the earth; the main one I see ahead is described in Ezekiel 38, which signifies the rise of Russia to a new level of prominence and power, causing many Jewish people to return to Israel and a new hatred against Israel to rise. Russia will align with Iran and other key nations in the Middle East, which will begin moving toward occupying Israel and establishing a different type of rule on the Temple Mount.

This is also a sign of the spirit of Cain arising throughout the earth. Cain signifies a form of godliness by denying power. As a form of religion, it will rise to persecute new forms of worship in days ahead. We must be very aware of these times and the rising forces that oppose us. Cain hated the true form of firstfruits worship and opened a door of iniquity. Nations, cities and societies were created out of Cain's choice not to worship God the way He deserved. Nations that have the spirit of Cain will align against the Lord—they are the goat nations that oppose Him and reject Israel.

Can Nations Realign to God's Perfect Plan?

Many other nations will be healed and become the sheep nations of the future. Isaiah 66:7–9 says,

> "Before she was in labor, she gave birth; before her pain came, she delivered a male child. Who has heard such a thing? Who has seen such things? Shall the earth be made to give birth

in one day? Or shall a nation be born at once? For as soon as Zion was in labor, she gave birth to her children. Shall I bring to the time of birth, and not cause delivery?" says the LORD. "Shall I who cause delivery shut up the womb?" says your God.

If God can birth a nation in a day, He can change a nation when it strays. Of course, this is linked with our covenant relation to Him. Isaiah also says that the nations are as a drop in the bucket to the Lord (Isaiah 40:15). They are no more difficult to deal with than individuals.

Restoration, however, is a different process than conception and birth. Since the Garden of Eden, people have been in need of restoration from the time they are born. God knits us together in our mothers' wombs, and I believe He knits our purposes within us. I also believe He knits His ability to press past every plan of the enemy that would stop us from coming into those purposes. When we rely on His ability, we overcome the enemy's plan.

God's ultimate intent was for the Garden to be filled with His glory, which would then work its way out and cover the entire earth. This is still His purpose, but now we are working from a standpoint of restoration. Land needs glory to represent the fullness of God. When a people align a nation with God's covenant plan, they start the restoration process of bringing God's glory into the earth realm. But when they divert from God's covenant plan, the glory lifts and decay begins. Therefore, we must process other elements before restoration occurs; we must deal with illegal bloodshed, idolatry, immorality and covenant breaking. Any time these issues enter into God's covenant relationship and plan for a nation, they have to be addressed and reconciliation has to occur.

Repent therefore and be converted, that your sins may be blotted out, so that times of refreshing may come from the presence of the Lord, and that He may send Jesus Christ, who was preached to you before, whom heaven must receive until the times of *restoration* of all things, which God has spoken by the mouth of all His holy prophets since the world began.

Acts 3:19–21 (emphasis added)

When Jesus ascended to the right hand of the Father, He left the Holy Spirit to be His agent of reconciliation. The Holy Spirit shakes us and convicts us of communion blocks— those things that prevent us from touching and talking with God. He first restores our ability to contact God. Then He restores every thing and place. We move from grief to glory. This comes when God begins to visit us in the place that He has determined for us.

When the true manifest presence of God visits humans, His glory radiates from that presence. At times God visibly displays His glory, often seen as fire or dazzling light, perhaps as a cloud or mist or sometimes as an act of His mighty power. Even when we do not visibly see manifestations of God's glory, the visitation leaves us with an impression of His glory burned into our hearts. It is the inward hidden work in our hearts that produces the Christlike attributes that move us from glory to glory.

The dictionary definition of restoration is "to revive and return to life" or "to bring back to a former or original condition." This definition falls short of all that restoration means. God intends to do more than bring us back to a former or original condition. Restoration begets multiplication! When you study the process of restoration, you discover that once it begins, you have the right to double, quadruple and even enter into a sevenfold completion of all God's purposes.

The promises of God are "Yes" and "Amen." This leads us to a triumphant confession that His people must make. We must know down deep that a nation can shift:

- *If* a remnant arises.
- *If* we are willing to war to receive God's covenant blessing.
- *If* we find our place in the gap. Nehemiah is a great example (Nehemiah 1–2). He received God's burden and found favor from the king to accomplish the task.
- *If* the Church is willing to shift from its discipling-teaching mentality to an apostolic-sending mentality (see John 20–21). Jesus discipled the Twelve until it was time to send them. Then He released them and sent them.
- *If* we allow the Spirit of God to align us in God's order. We find an order of God in 1 Corinthians 12:28: first apostles, second prophets. When God says "first," He is showing the prototype of the future. When apostles and prophets align in our region, then teachers and pastors will rise up with new anointing, and we will see miracles and healings that unlock evangelism.
- *If* we will allow the Lord to shake disinterest, confusion, legalism, condemnation, discouragement and disillusionment. Once God began to shake the people in the days of Haggai, He assured them that their latter would be greater than their former. He shook them into a desire to complete His purposes (Haggai 1–2).
- *If* we are willing to be like the woman at the well, dropping our pots and running quickly (John 4). This woman tore down her prejudices, overcame her past, experienced a new reality of the Lord, left her mundane

daily exercise of getting water and ran to evangelize her entire city.

- *If* we are willing to bind the strongman who has robbed us of our spoils. In Matthew 12:25–29, we find that we should first bind the strongman, and *then* go in and take his spoils. We are entering into a season of plundering the enemy's camp.

Can a nation be changed, even in a day? The answer is *yes*! I repeat, the promises of God are "Yes" and "Amen." Shout, "*Yes!*" and see your nation realign and shift into God's purposes!

The Lord told Joshua, "Every place that the sole of your foot will tread upon I have given you, as I said to Moses" (Joshua 1:3), and He later reiterated it: "Be strong and of good courage, for to this people you shall divide as an inheritance the land which I swore to their fathers to give them" (verse 6). In other words, when you are moving forward, you first need to know what God has said about the land you are moving onto. Once you know that, you have a responsibility to realign and rearrange heaven and earth on that land. When you do that, something will shift!

Large Enough to Receive His Fullness

He came that we might be full of Him! *Fullness* is a time word, though we often do not associate the two. When bowls are filled, all the parts are added up and everything that must be reconciled is reconciled—that is fullness. Fullness also means He must have a structure or container to fill. The earth is the Lord's container to fill with His glory. In each generation, however, He creates different structures to assist Him in pouring out this glory. He fills until His plan is fulfilled (see John 1:16). And He fills *until we run over!* The Spirit of God does not just fill to the brim; He fills until the structure runs over, pours out and covers the place assigned.

A place of abundance is available to us (see John 10:10) in which this filling occurs. Look around you and see if things are filling up with His glory. Fullness is linked with life, and life means movement, for in Him, we move and have our being (see Acts 17:24–28; Colossians 1:19; 2:9). The fuller we are with His Spirit, the better we move.

He needs a vessel to fill or bring to completion (see Matthew 9:16–17; Mark 2:21–22; 6:43; 8:20). God knows when one new man has developed. It will occur when the salvation of the Gentiles has reached a number that satisfies God's requirement for completeness (see Romans 11:12, 25). Then the Jews start experiencing salvation. The two, Jew and Gentile, start becoming one to reflect God's Kingdom plan in the earth. In the Jews' rejection of the Messiah, a door opened for salvation to come to the Gentiles. God loves people and He created Israel and the Jews, and His plan of fullness is now working to bring the salvation of the Gentile and Jew into overflowing.

The measure of Christ's blessing can overflow in us (see Romans 15:29), in the earth, and in time (see Ephesians 1:10; Galatians 4:4). His love for us is so deep that we cannot measure it using the world's measurements (see Ephesians 3:18–19). God's sovereign appointment of events is linked with His plan to restore and produce fullness, as is His divine nature maturing in us (see Colossians 2:9). His plan of fullness is linked with His visitation from generation to generation.

As believers mature in their faith, they come into unity with Him. For this to occur, His government must be established.

Therefore, the development of our thinking and the structure that holds and manifests that thinking process is linked with His plan of fullness in the earth! When Jesus was ascending to the right hand of Father God to make Himself available to us in this age, He gave gifts, knowing that we would have to allow gifts to develop in the earth that could govern the earth.

God with Us

In days ahead, knowing the presence of God will be the key to our lives. His name is Immanuel, God with us! His presence will direct us.

The name *Immanuel* appears twice in the Hebrew Scriptures and once in the New Testament. It first appears in Isaiah 7:14 as part of a prophetic word that Isaiah spoke to King Ahaz of Judah (the southern kingdom) at a time when Syria and Israel (the northern kingdom) had formed a coalition against Assyria. Isaiah counseled Ahaz not to join in Israel's uprising against Assyria, the region's greatest power, urging Ahaz to trust in the Lord instead. To confirm the word, Isaiah said, "the Lord himself will give you this sign: A virgin will become pregnant and give birth to a son, and she will name him Immanuel" (Isaiah 7:14 GW). Shortly after that, Syria and Israel were soundly defeated, as Isaiah had prophesied.

Matthew's gospel recalls Isaiah's prophecy, applying it to the child born of the virgin betrothed to Joseph. The sign given hundreds of years earlier to an apostate king was meant for all God's people. One of the most comforting of all the names and titles of Jesus, it is literally translated "with us is God" or, as Matthew puts it, "God with us." In fact, the Bible is nothing if not the story of God's persistent desire to dwell with His people. In Jesus, God would succeed in a unique way, becoming a man in order to save the world not from the outside but from the inside. Immanuel, God with us, to rescue, redeem and restore our relationship with Him. The only way we will triumph in days ahead is to know God-with-us and grow in discernment.

Conflict is coming. We will find many confrontations in our path. Like Moses, we will ask, "'Who am I that I should go to Pharaoh and bring the people of Israel out of Egypt?' Elohim answered, 'I will be with you'" (Exodus 3:11–12 NOG). Emmanuel is the God who never abandons us. He said to Joshua, "I will never neglect you or abandon you. . . . I have commanded you, 'Be strong and courageous! Don't tremble or be terrified, because Yahweh your Elohim is with you wherever you go'" (Joshua 1:5, 9 NOG). Through Isaiah, He said, "When you go through the sea, I am with you. When you go through rivers, they will not sweep you away. When you walk through fire, you will not be burned, and the flames will not harm you" (Isaiah 43:2 NOG). And to His disciples, Jesus said, "And remember that I am always with you until the end of time" (Matthew 28:20 NOG).

Similarly we must come to know the name *Jehovah Shammah*, "in your captivity I am there." We must know His presence as we journey through times of conflict.

You Must Choose This Day!

I want to conclude by saying that I believe we are living in a time like that at the end of the book of Joshua. We must make choices. We can increase our stability and confidence in decision making. We must determine what, how and when to build for the future. Ask and receive a new anointing to optimize resources and do exploits. Embrace His mind for increase and multiplication. Define and develop a frame of reference in changing times. Declare that stalemates from the last season will break and you will go to the next level of maturity. Reverse Satan's strategies of manipulation, through which he changed your time and law. Steward what you have been given so you can multiply and be given entire cities to rule (see Luke 19:11–27). Organize, decode and activate the necessary strategies to remove the taunting aspects of uncertainty in your future. Control your fears, and do not allow them to control you.

Lawlessness will have many avenues throughout the world. Indeed, we have seen lawlessness increase greatly. In an effort to control this chaos, many laws have been established that will severely restrict our freedom.

Governments of the world cannot fully change until the government of God on earth aligns itself and represents the order of God. That means leaders in the Church must get their act together! I see many denominations or wineskins of the past fading and becoming irrelevant. We have already seen many changes. We are aware of God's foundational plan of apostles, prophets, evangelists, pastors and teachers. We are learning how to interact with each other. We are letting go of old methods of operation and embracing new ways of worship.

A triumphant reserve is arising! The real war to come will manifest in how we fellowship. We will have to learn how to operate in decentralized fellowship. In other words, we will not all be going to church every Sunday. That form of worship is changing rapidly. At the same time, corporate worship gatherings in certain territories will break through into new levels of revelation. I am not talking about extrabiblical revelation, since the Bible already has been canonized; it is the established Word of God. Rather, I believe revelation is coming that will cause the Word to become even more applicable for this age, while also giving us strategies to defeat the enemy. Many of what are now corporate warfare-worship gatherings will turn into times of travail, and the result will be changed nations. As we come together and worship in such settings, we will gain new strategies for how to govern in our spheres of authority.

The Lord of Hosts, Yahweh Sabaoth—captain of all the angelic armies, the armies of Israel and the hosts of nations, ruler of everything in heaven and on earth—sends help on our behalf. The King then accesses our lives, cities, corporate worship or nations. When we worship, He begins to order and align His armies for victory. "Hosts" signifies an organized group under authority. God has a multitude of ready and able servants. We must remain a peculiar people ready to do God's will (from heaven) in the land that we occupy here in the earth. We represent God in our nations. As the Body of Christ, we should be the driving force in maintaining freedom in the earth. The Body of Christ should rise up and say, "Let us return and be restored to the Lord."

"Fear not, for I am with you; be not dismayed, for I am your God. I will strengthen you, yes, I will help you, I will uphold you with My righteous right hand. . . . Those who war against you shall be as nothing . . . 'Fear not, I will help you'" (Isaiah 41:10, 12–13). This is a time to understand the power of violence and become violent in the Spirit by praising God in new ways. This will be a season of violence. A season of intense learning. A season of falling and getting back up. A season to overcome fear. A season to learn a different way of prospering financially.

We must allow the Lord to discipline and make us watchmen. You must know who you are watching after and are connected with, and you must know who is watching after you. Get your assignment quickly. We must understand signs in this season that identify and uncover godliness and the redemptive plan of God in the world. We must not miss our signs at this time! We must not be afraid of the supernatural, but rather enter into that dimension that will get us to our new "there." This will begin individually and develop into a corporate demonstration.

In this season we will begin to interpret supernatural revelation. We must ask God for the gift of interpretation. The Lord will be releasing a new revelation in the earth realm so we understand times and seasons. Dreams will become very significant, and there will be a revival of words of knowledge. Words of wisdom will give us clear, directive strategy for the words of knowledge we receive. These two gifts will balance each other (for more understanding, read Daniel 6–11).

There will be much shifting in the Church and in lands of the earth at this time. Many will become dissatisfied with traditionalism and will seek God's supernatural power. Therefore, God will shift many into new places. On the other hand, many in the Body of Christ are critical, judgmental, negative and condemning. Unless they are delivered, they will wander in this next season, unable to find their places. If we will pray Isaiah 58 and let God lead us into the type of fast that He has for each of us, we will be delivered and positioned properly for the future. Realign yourself! God is changing territorial boundaries.

The Lord is ready to bring an end to certain curses in the land. He will show us how to end curses, and Joel 2 will be very important. This is a year to transfer evil into blessing.

Do not be afraid to face the curse that has hindered your progress. Decode the occult structure linked with the curse. Evaluate its destruction, and begin the rebuilding cycle for your future.

We can prosper on the new, treacherous path ahead. As we advance, new light advances before us. The Lord will begin to penetrate ungodly nations and bring His glory to places that have never experienced Him. This will be a season of pioneering into new places after judgment and wrath have occurred.

We will begin to face the antichrist system designed to hinder God's Kingdom advancing in the earth realm. Fear not and tread forth!

We will experience a type of worship different than we have ever known. The Tabernacle of David is being established. Individual worship will turn into corporate worship, the key to transforming our regions. This is a season when the roar of the Lion becomes very distinguishable. The enemy will roar loudly, but the Lion of Judah will roar louder still. We must learn the Lion of Judah's sound. It is in us, and it must be drawn out of us. Ferret out criminals. Psalm 101 is a key chapter; pray this for your region, and that every evil thing will be exposed.

We must learn to stand and withstand. Ephesians 6:10–18 (emphasis added) says,

> Finally, my brethren, be strong in the Lord and in the power of His might. Put on the whole armor of God, that you may be able to *stand* against the wiles of the devil. For we do not wrestle against flesh and blood, but against principalities, against powers, against the rulers of the darkness of this age, against spiritual hosts of wickedness in the heavenly places. Therefore take up the whole armor of God, that you may

be able to *withstand* in the evil day, and having done all, to *stand*. *Stand* therefore, having girded your waist with truth, having put on the breastplate of righteousness, and having shod your feet with the preparation of the gospel of peace; above all, taking the shield of faith with which you will be able to quench all the fiery darts of the wicked one. And take the helmet of salvation, and the sword of the Spirit, which is the word of God; praying always with all prayer and supplication in the Spirit, being watchful to this end with all perseverance and supplication for all the saints.

James 4:7–8 admonishes us, "Therefore submit to God. Resist the devil and he will flee from you. Draw near to God and He will draw near to you. Cleanse your hands, you sinners; and purify your hearts, you double-minded."

To stand and withstand, we must be anointed. Isaiah 10:27 proclaims that the anointing breaks the yoke! The Hebrew word *mashiach* [Messiah] refers to one who is anointed with oil, symbolizing the reception of the Holy Spirit, enabling him to do an assigned task. Kings (1 Samuel 24:6), high priests and some prophets (1 Kings 19:16) were anointed. Cyrus was commissioned to be the "anointed deliverer" of Israel (see Isaiah 45:1). The patriarchs were called "anointed ones." As I said earlier, we need to receive a new anointing. This anointing will give you victory over death cycles and the fear of death. May you be anointed to have victory over demonic forces that would try to stop you in the future. May you be anointed for increase and harvest so you begin to fill His storehouse. May you have an Issachar anointing to interpret the times so you know what decisions to make.

Appendix

An Analysis
of the Seven Churches
# of Revelation

Which One Are You?[1]

EPHESUS

The Church That Lost Its Fervent Love

The first church addressed in Revelation 2 is the church at Ephesus, the church that has departed from its first love. Ephesus had been a brightly burning lampstand. Jesus commended those in the Ephesian church for seven things:

- Their living faith (their deeds)
- Their diligence (their toil)
- Their standards (they did not tolerate evil)

- Their discernment (they tested apostles to see who was true)
- Their perseverance (they kept going despite opposition)
- Their endurance (they were in it for the long haul)
- Their strength (they had not grown weary)

But the Ephesian church had a problem: Somehow, in the midst of all their work, they had lost the *love* of God they had once known. They still did a lot of good things, but the fervent love that once motivated them was no longer there. The result was that their lampstand had begun to go out! Because of this, Jesus gave them a warning: "I will come to you quickly and remove your lampstand from its place—unless you repent" (Revelation 2:5). All the work in the world counts for nothing if you have lost your love.

Jesus then showed them the path to restoration. To regain what they had lost, they needed to do three things:

1. Remember from where they had fallen.
2. Repent . . . to *change* their direction.
3. Do the deeds they did at first.

SMYRNA

The Persecuted Church

Smyrna was a large and prosperous city, a seat of learning and culture. The Smyrnans were proud of their city and had a fanatical loyalty to Rome. Within this culture, the highest form of worship was worshiping the Roman emperor. The Smyrnans had no tolerance for those who would not worship the emperor. As a result, the church there suffered for its faith. In Mark 10:29–30, Jesus promised that, along with many blessings, we would receive persecutions. The church at Smyrna had experienced that persecution and was about to suffer more.

But Jesus had a promise for His persecuted church: "Do not fear any of those things which you are about to suffer. . . . He who overcomes shall not be hurt by the second death" (Revelation 2:10–11). Jesus assured them that, while they may face suffering and even *physical* death, they had *eternal* life. Essentially, His message to Smyrna was, "In the midst of persecution, *be faithful!*" Jesus identified Himself to them as the One "who was dead, and came to life" (verse 8). He was reminding them that death is not the end: "If you are faithful, you will receive a victor's crown!" Even if you suffer in this life, it is worth it to follow Jesus. If you die for your faith, you have still won!

PERGAMOS

The Unfaithful Church

Pergamos was a center of paganism. On the hill above the city was the Pergamos acropolis, crowded with pagan temples. The most striking feature of the acropolis was a huge temple shaped like a giant throne. It was the altar to Zeus, ruler of all the Greek gods.

Jesus' message to the church in Pergamos began with "I know your works, and where you dwell, where Satan's throne is" (Revelation 2:13). False gods are demons, which means worship of false gods is worship of demons. Zeus, as the ruler of false gods, represents the head of demons, Satan. Thus above the city of Pergamos was a huge throne dedicated to

269

the devil! Jesus added that their city was "where Satan dwells" (verse 13). As the worship of God brings God's presence, so the worship of Zeus in Pergamos caused Satan's presence to dwell in a discernable way. This church was called to stand in a hard place, and Jesus immediately acknowledged that they had held fast to His name.

Unfortunately, Jesus also had some issues with their current state. They had fallen into the trap of the Nicolaitans. These were false teachers who perverted the idea of freedom in Christ. Because we are free in Christ, they taught, why should we invite persecution by being legalistic? Pagan gods do not exist, after all. It does not hurt to eat at a pagan feast, or to put incense on an altar . . .

The Christians at Pergamos had been seduced by this teaching. They compromised with the pagan world, even joining in feasts honoring demons! Jesus compared this to the trap set for Israel by Balaam. If joining in pagan feasts is the equivalent of fornication, to be seduced by the world is adultery. As a result, Jesus warned this church harshly: "Repent, or else I will come to you quickly and will fight against them with the sword of My mouth" (verse 16). Thankfully, Jesus also promised a reward to those who would repent.

THYATIRA

A Church Invaded by a Religious Spirit

Thyatira was known for its purple dye and fabrics and was home to corporate guilds of potters, tanners, weavers, dyers and robe makers. To hold membership in these guilds, one had to feast at the temple of Apollo, the site of guild business dinners that were usually followed by orgies. This obviously made it difficult for Christians to prosper in Thyatira.

Jesus' issue with the church was this: An influential woman in the church had identified herself as a prophet and justified the practice of fornication, idol worship and eating of meat sacrificed to idols, and the church tolerated it (Revelation 2:20). We can presume this false teaching was welcomed because it allowed church members to join the guilds. It is interesting that Jesus never said exactly *what* this woman's teaching was; He simply identified the spirit behind it—that of Jezebel!

In certain church circles, the term *Jezebel* is tossed around frequently, but many believers do not accurately understand the Jezebel spirit. It is not a "female" spirit. (Many men have a Jezebel spirit.) It does not always work behind the scenes. What actually characterizes a Jezebel spirit is that it is *always* religious. A Jezebel spirit seeks a position of influence among God's people so it can promote a false system of religion. Here are some characteristics of this spirit:

- A Jezebel spirit seeks to draw God's people into false religion of any kind.
- It operates through control, false teaching, manipulation and intimidation.
- It often identifies itself as a defender of the faith and promotes false prophets.
- It opposes the Holy Spirit and all of His manifestations.
- It hates the true prophetic word and persecutes God's prophets.

A Jezebel spirit is a mean spirit that shows no mercy. In this passage, Jesus personally decreed judgment on Jezebel. To those who had not followed her, He had a word of encouragement: "Hold fast what you have till I come" (verse 25). Thyatira was a good church. It did not have many problems—apart from Jezebel! Simply put, Jesus was saying, "Deal with her and you'll do great! Keep moving forward!"

SARDIS

The Comfortable Church

Sardis was one of the most pleasant places to live in the ancient world. It was a center of worldwide trade and one of most affluent cities in the world. Life was easy in Sardis. Even in the pagan world, Sardis had a reputation for materialism and decadence. The pagans there were extremely accepting and did not care if you worshiped their gods or not. They just wanted to make money and have a good time.

The church in Sardis was also comfortable. There is no mention of persecution or opposition whatsoever, no issue of false teaching or heresy. They were contented and well-off . . . yet Jesus had nothing good to say about this church! He told them, "I know your works, that you have a name that you are alive, but you are dead" (Revelation 3:1). Ouch! In other words, Jesus was saying, "You have an appearance of life—you *look* good. You are doing lots of good things, but there's no *life*!" The church at Sardis was the church of the living dead!

They had become too attached to the world. Their hearts were captured by the affluence in Sardis, and they loved its luxuries. Jesus' exhortation to the church at Sardis was to *wake up*! "Strengthen the things which remain, that are ready to die, for I have not found your works perfect before God" (verse 2). Sardis was not all dead, but it was losing strength fast. Jesus then told the people, "Remember therefore how you have received and heard; hold fast and repent" (verse 3). They did not need a new message; they needed to hold on to what they received, turn back and get on the right path.

Jesus warned the Christians in Sardis that He would come to examine His church. The word He used actually suggests an audit. If they remained as they were, they would forfeit their destiny. But if they woke up and overcame, they would take their part in ministry among His priests, and He would confess them before the Father and all the angels.

PHILADELPHIA

The Church of God's Favor

Philadelphia was located on the Royal Road, the main east-west trade route into the interior of Asia. Because of this, it was built as a "missionary" city, designed as a showplace for Greek civilization in Asia and to spread Greek language, culture and religion to the barbarians of the east. In fact, it had so many temples, it was known as "little Athens."

In 17 AD, a massive earthquake struck and the city was literally destroyed overnight. Emperor Tiberius rebuilt the city and restored its beauty, but massive aftershocks continued to hit the city for decades. The result was that the majority of its people lived in the surrounding countryside. Few were brave enough to live in the shaky city.

The Philadelphia church had also experienced shaking through seasons of persecution. They had been through a hard season, and they felt weakened. But Jesus had the most positive word given to any of the seven churches: "You have suffered for your faith, but you persevered—and that is very important to God! You kept My Word and did not deny My name. You endured patiently. And because you have remained steadfast, God has opened a door for you that no one can close." In short, Philadelphia had passed the test and, as a result, now had a golden opportunity.

For the Philadelphians, this included an open door to their city. They had been falsely accused, and their reputation in the city had been tarnished. Yet Jesus promised vindication: Even their enemies would acknowledge that God was with them. Their open door was also one to the entire world. Philadelphia was called to be a missionary city for the Church, as well. Through the Church, Philadelphia would begin to fulfill its destiny as a gateway to the world.

Philadelphia indeed became a gateway city for the Gospel: Missionaries went out on the Royal Road and established thriving churches in Persia, India and even as far as China.

LAODICEA

The Lukewarm Church

Laodicea was a major trade center and banking capital. It was built on the crossroads of several trade routes, and its banking system and the many caravans that came through made it a wealthy city. It was also an important medical center. Built at the foot of a volcanic mountain known for its hot mineral springs, the city featured health spas where the sick came for treatment. Jesus described His relationship with this church in Revelation 3:20: "Behold, I stand at the door and knock. If anyone hears My voice and opens the door, I will come in to him and dine with him, and he with Me."

That is probably the most famous verse in Revelation. We frequently talk about Jesus "knocking on the door" of an unbeliever's heart. Yet few Christians really understand that, in context, Jesus was not knocking on an unbeliever's heart—He was knocking on the door of His church! It is important that we understand this picture. Revelation 2 and 3 show Jesus moving from church to church, tending His lamps to keep them burning brightly. He approaches each one to correct and encourage. But when he comes to Laodicea, *He cannot get in!*

Other churches had problems, but Laodicea had gone a step further. Something about the church at Laodicea *shut the door* to Jesus coming into their church. Jesus described the problem in Laodicea in one word: *lukewarm.*

If anyone understood what it meant to be lukewarm, it was the Laodiceans. The hot springs on the mountain were wonderful for the health spas, but by the time the water flowed through the aqueducts to the city, it had cooled off. The city's water was lukewarm mineral water, considered almost undrinkable. In fact, it was nauseating! Jesus said to the believers of Laodicea, "Your church is like your water!" He then added a surprising twist: "I wish you were cold or hot."

To be cold is to reject Jesus, yet Jesus can deal with rejection. If you are cold to Him, it just means you have never known His love. The truth is, there is great hope for those who are cold. When they see who He really is, they can quickly change from cold to hot. On the other extreme, to be hot is to be on fire for Jesus, madly and passionately in love. That is what Jesus is looking for! That is what He deserves. He gave Himself completely for us, and He wants us to give our hearts completely to Him.

The Laodiceans were neither cold nor hot. They were lukewarm—about as middle of the road as you can get. They did not oppose Jesus, but they were not excited about Him, either. They were *indifferent* to the One who gave His life for them. To that attitude, Jesus' response was harsher than any of His other messages to the churches: "I will vomit you out of My mouth" (verse 16). Vomiting is a violent, *involuntary* reaction to something that is totally unpalatable. It is a knee-jerk, *natural* response that requires no thinking. Here Jesus is saying, "Lukewarm Christianity makes Me want to puke!" That is what kept the door closed to Jesus; He could not come into a church like that.

But Jesus did not give up on Laodicea. He was still knocking at the door, calling out for someone to open it. In fact, the Lord had high hopes for it: "If you will open the door, I will come in!" Their solution was to gain a new perspective on life. They thought they were rich and needed nothing. Jesus' response? "[You] do not know that you are wretched, miserable, poor, blind, and naked—I counsel you to buy from Me gold refined in the fire, that you may be rich; and white garments, that you may be clothed, that the shame of your nakedness may not be revealed; and anoint your eyes with eye salve, that you may see" (verses 17–18).

Jesus wanted the Laodiceans to see their need and come to Him as their source. He promised that if they would open the door to His presence, He would be faithful to come in. They would feast with Him! Not only would they feast with Him, Revelation 3:21 guarantees that if they overcame in the battle before them, they would gain a place on His throne. Jesus' word to Laodicea was simply this: "It's a battle to break out of the lukewarm. But if you overcome, You will gain great authority in the earth. *You will reign with Me!*"

Notes

Chapter 1: A Prophetic Portal into the Future

1. These books that help the Body understand the time of war in which we live are *The Worship Warrior* (Regal, 2002), *Restoring Your Shield of Faith* (Regal, 2004), *God's Unfolding Battle Plan* (Chosen, 2007), *Worship as It Is in Heaven* (Regal, 2010), *Time to Defeat the Devil* (Charisma House, 2011) and *The Apostolic Church Arising* (Glory of Zion International, 2015).

2. Dutch Sheets, *God's Timing for Your Life* (Ventura, Calif.: Regal, 2001), 16–17.

3. Arthur Burk, *Relentless Generational Blessings* (Anaheim, Calif.: Plumbline Ministries, 2003).

4. What follows is adapted from Chuck D. Pierce, Rebecca Wagner Sytsema, *The Future War of the Church* (Ventura, Calif.: Regal, 2001; reissued Minneapolis: Chosen, 2007), 80–82.

5. Ernest B. Gentile, *Worship God!* (Portland: City Bible Publishing, 1994), 90.

6. Sheets, *God's Timing for Your Life*, 17–18.

7. Chuck D. Pierce and Rebecca Wagner Sytsema, *God's Now Time for Your Life* (Ventura, Calif.: Regal, 2005), 16.

8. Chuck D. Pierce and John Dickson, *The Worship Warrior* (Ventura, Calif.: Regal, 2002), 230.

9. Pierce and Sytsema, *Future War of the Church*, 65–66.

10. Ibid., 66.

11. Pierce and Dickson, *The Worship Warrior*, 230–231.

Chapter 2: Shifting into the War Ahead

1. In this segment of Church history, two champions of the restorative move of God arose, Dr. C. Peter Wagner and Prophet Bill Hamon. Both have written numerous books to capture the history of this shift. Therefore, I will not elaborate

on the shift that has occurred but focus instead on the *now* results. Here are several books that will help you learn how to align yourself in this movement.

By C. Peter Wagner: *This Changes Everything* (Chosen, 2013); *On Earth As It Is in Heaven* (Regal, 2012); *Dominion* (Chosen, 2008); *Apostles Today* (Regal, 2007); *Changing Church* (Regal, 2004); *Spheres of Authority* (Regal, 2002); *Apostles and Prophets* (Regal, 2000); *Churchquake* (Regal, 1999); *The New Apostolic Church* (Regal, 1998). By Bishop Bill Hamon: *The Day of the Saints* (Destiny Image, 2002); *The Eternal Church* (Destiny Image, 2003); *Apostles, Prophets and the Coming Moves of God* (Destiny Image, 1997).

Chuck D. Pierce and Robert Heidler, *The Apostolic Church Arising* (Glory of Zion International Ministries, 2015). Robert Heidler, *The Messianic Church Arising* (Glory of Zion International Ministries, 2006).

2. Adapted from Chuck D. Pierce, *Redeeming the Time* (Lake Mary, Fla.: Charisma House, 2009), 19–21.

3. What follows is adapted from Pierce and Sytsema, *Future War of the Church*, 31–34.

4. For further study, you should have in your possession a unique book by Robert and Linda Heidler and myself, *A Time to Advance: Understanding the Significance of the Hebrew Tribes and Months* (Glory of Zion International, 2011).

5. Robert M. Haralick, *The Inner Meaning of the Hebrew Letters* (Northdale, N.J.: Jason Aronson, Inc., 1995), 129–130.

6. Ibid., 72–73.

7. *International Standard Bible Encyclopaedia* (Chicago: Howard-Severance Company, 1915), s.v. "Issachar."

8. Andrew R. Fausset, *Fausset's Bible Dictionary* (1949), s.v. "Issachar," http ://www.studylight.org/dictionaries/fbd/view.cgi?n=1827.

Chapter 3: A New Mindskin for a New Wineskin

1. Jerry Tuma, "How the Economy Will Continue to Shift" (presentation at How to Succeed in a Season of Rearranging Economic Structures, Denton, Texas, July 6, 2009).

2. Harold R. Eberle, *The Complete Wineskin*, 4th ed. (Yakima, Wash.: Winepress Publishing, 1997), 1–2.

3. Graham Cooke, *A Divine Confrontation* (Shippensburg, Pa.: Destiny Image, 1999), 285.

4. The following is adapted from Chuck D. Pierce and Robert Heidler, *The Apostolic Church Arising* (Denton, Tex.: Glory of Zion International Ministries, 2015), 9–16.

Chapter 4: Why Christians Must Learn War

1. Peter C. Craigie, *The Problem of War in the Old Testament* (Grand Rapids, Mich.: Eerdmans, 1978), 11.

2. John Eckhardt, *Fasting for Breakthrough and Deliverance* (Lake Mary, Fla.: Charisma House, 2016), 1–2.

3. List of five operations is adapted from Chuck D. Pierce, *God's Unfolding Battle Plan* (Minneapolis: Chosen, 2007), 33–35.
4. Pierce and Sytsema, *Future War of the Church*, 57.
5. Cindy Jacobs, *Women of Destiny* (Ventura, Calif.: Regal, 1998), 153.

Chapter 5: Authority to Overthrow Iniquitous Thrones

1. I have explained some of these in other books; one that may help you is *Protecting Your Home from Spiritual Darkness* (Chosen, 2004).
2. Chuck D. Pierce, *Time to Defeat the Devil* (Lake Mary, Fla.: Charisma Media, 2011), 67.
3. Pierce, *Time to Defeat the Devil*, 68–69.

Chapter 6: A Triumphant Army Arising

1. We wrote an account of this fifty-state tour in *Releasing the Prophetic Destiny of a Nation* (Destiny Image, 2005).
2. Delivered at the U.S. Global Apostolic Prayer Network leadership meeting in Denton, Texas, January 8, 2006.
3. In *The Apostolic Church Arising*, Dr. Robert Heidler and I communicate the history of apostolic centers in the Bible (e.g., Jerusalem, Antioch and Corinth) and reveal the shift to come from Church to Kingdom.

Chapter 7: Overcomers of the Covenant War

1. Joseph H. Hellerman, *The Ancient Church as Family* (Minneapolis: Fortress Press, 2001), 51, 58.
2. Ibid., 58.
3. Ibid.
4. Ibid., 43.
5. Kevin Conner and Ken Malmin, *The Covenants* (Portland: City Bible Publishing, 1983), i.
6. Ibid., 73–74. The following list of Scripture references is adapted from Connor and Malmin: forgiveness and remission of the penalty of sin (Acts 10:43; 13:36–39), justification and righteousness (Romans 5:1; 3:24–26), being born again into the family of God (Matthew 6:9; John 3:1–5; 1 Peter 1:23), assurance (Hebrews 5:8–9; 6:10–12; 10:38–39; 1 John 3:19), sanctification to the Lord (John 17:17; Ephesians 5:26–27; 1 Thessalonians 5:23–24), adoption as sons and daughters of God (Romans 8:15–23; Galatians 4:5; Ephesians 1:13–14), and glorification (John 17:22–24; Romans 8:17–30; 2 Corinthians 3:18).
7. Ibid., 95–96. The following list of Scripture references is adapted from Connor and Malmin: everlasting life (Daniel 12:2; Matthew 19:29; Luke 18:30; John 3:16, 36; 4:14; 5:24; 6:27, 40, 47; 12:50; Acts 13:46; Romans 6:22; Galatians 6:8; 1 Timothy 6:16), immortality (Romans 2:7; 1 Corinthians 15:15–57; 2 Corinthians 5:1–5; 1 Timothy 6:16; 2 Timothy 1:9–10), an everlasting kingdom which the believer inherits (Psalm 145:13; Daniel 4:3, 34; 7:14, 27; Matthew 25:34; 1 Corinthians 6:9–10; Galatians 5:21; Ephesians 5:5; 2 Peter 1:11), eternal inheritance (Hebrews 9:14), everlasting love, kindness and mercy (Psalms 100:5; 103:17; Isaiah

54:8; Jeremiah 31:3), everlasting righteousness (Daniel 9:24), everlasting habitations (Luke 16:9), everlasting joy (Isaiah 51:11; 61:7), everlasting strength (Isaiah 26:4), and an everlasting name (Isaiah 56:5; 63:12, 16). Scripture references for promises for overcomers include being given the eternal tree of life (Revelation 2:7), not being hurt by death (Revelation 2:11), receiving hidden manna and a white stone with a new name in it (Revelation 2:17), power over the nations, ruling and reigning with Jesus over all enemies (Revelation 2:26–28), being clothed with white raiment of light and having one's name confessed before the Father and the angels (Revelation 3:4–5), being a pillar in the temple of God (Revelation 3:12), sitting with Jesus on His throne (Revelation 3:21), and inheriting all things (Revelation 21:7).

8. Bob Beckett, *Commitment to Conquer* (Grand Rapids, Mich.: Chosen, 1997), 85–86.

Chapter 8: The War over One New Man

1. This exhortation was shared on April 26, 2016.

Chapter 9: The War of Religion

1. This is plainly evident in the life of Dr. C. Peter Wagner, a man filled with joy (and it has been one of the great joys of my life to work alongside him). He enjoys people, his life, his family, his ministry and his own jokes. Peter never lets life get stale and rob him of joy. I believe that a key to his life is his *love for embracing change*. In recent history, when God decided it was time to bring change into the earthly realm through new thought processes, Peter has always seemed to be one of the first to raise his hand and say, "Use me!" He has compiled a series of essays into a great book called *Freedom from the Religious Spirit* (Regal, 2005).

2. I wrote a great chapter on this with Rebecca Wagner Sytsema in *Possessing Your Inheritance* (Regal, 1999).

Chapter 10: What Will Become of Me?

1. When Robert Heidler, one of the most profound and easy-to-understand theologians I know, teaches on the seven churches of Revelation, my spirit man leaps inside. His full teaching set, *How Is Your Lampstand Burning? Understanding the Seven Churches of Revelation*, is available from Glory of Zion International.

2. Dutch Sheets and Chuck D. Pierce, *Releasing the Prophetic Destiny of a Nation* (Shippensburg, Pa.: Destiny Image, 2005), 78–79.

3. Spiros Zodhiates, ed., *Hebrew-Greek Key Word Study Bible*, New American Standard Bible (Chattanooga: AMG Publishers, 1977), 1287.

4. Sheets and Pierce, *Prophetic Destiny*, 80.

5. C. Peter Wagner, *This Changes Everything* (Minneapolis: Chosen, 2013), 203–204. Used by permission of Chosen Books, a division of Baker Publishing Group.

6. Another dream she had on simplicity led to a book she and I wrote together. *The Rewards of Simplicity* (Chosen, 2010) gives great insight on how to prepare

for days ahead. Each chapter helps you receive healing from traumas of the past that cause you to face your future with anxiety.

7. Communicated on May 6, 2016.
8. Communicated on November 14, 2014.

Appendix: An Analysis of the Seven Churches of Revelation

1. Adapted from Robert Heidler, *How Is Your Lampstand Burning? Understanding the Seven Churches of Revelation* (Denton, Tex.: Glory of Zion International Ministries, 2006), CD series.

Charles D. "Chuck" Pierce serves as president of Global Spheres, Inc. (GSI), in Corinth, Texas. This is an apostolic, prophetic ministry that is being used to gather and mobilize the worshiping triumphant reserve throughout the world. GSI facilitates other ministries as well and participates in regional and national gatherings to develop new Kingdom paradigms. Peter and Doris Wagner complete the leadership team of this new wineskin. Chuck also serves as president of Glory of Zion International Ministries, a ministry that aligns Jew and Gentile. He is known for his accurate prophetic gifting, which helps direct nations, cities, churches and individuals in understanding the times and seasons in which we live. Chuck and his wife, Pam, have six children and ten grandchildren. He has authored and co-authored more than twenty books, including the bestsellers *Possessing Your Inheritance*, *The Future War of the Church*, *The Worship Warrior*, *God's Unfolding Battle Plan*, *Interpreting the Times*, *Redeeming the Time*, *Time to Defeat the Devil* and *The Apostolic Church Arising*.

More from Chuck D. Pierce

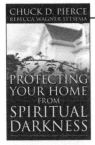

This practical guide shows you how to battle Satan on the final, most intimate frontier: your home. You'll discover ten simple steps to rid your home of spiritual darkness, lock out evil and turn your home into a fortress for Light.

Protecting Your Home from Spiritual Darkness
(with Rebecca Wagner Sytsema)

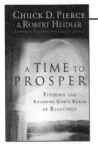

Discover the biblical model for work, worship and giving—and understand how this pattern prepares you to give and receive blessings. Now is the time to claim your inheritance and your portion and dwell in the realm of God's blessing.

A Time to Prosper (with Robert Heidler)

This prophetic vision from Chuck Pierce—now fully realized—offers a glimpse into the spiritual battle the Church is fighting today, as well as encouragement to triumph over the forces of lawlessness, hopelessness and violence. Learn how to be victorious through strategic intercession, worship warfare and a powerful weapon of intercession.

God's Unfolding Battle Plan

✔Chosen